ATKINS IS DEAD, PASS THE BREAD

Printed in the United States of America
by G&R Publishing Co.

Distributed By:

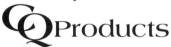Products

507 Industrial Street
Waverly, IA 50677

ISBN 1-56383-188-0
Item #7003

Table of Contents

Beverages
& Appetizers

Tomato Juice

Makes 2 quarts

12 medium tomatoes, cored
   and quartered
1/2 C. water
1/3 C. coarsely chopped
   onions
2 stalks celery, coarsely
   chopped

1 tsp. fresh minced
   parsley
1 bay leaf
1 1/4 tsp. salt
1/4 tsp. paprika
1/4 tsp. sugar

In a Dutch oven over medium heat, bring quartered tomatoes, water, chopped onions, chopped celery, minced parsley and bay leaf to a boil. Reduce heat, cover and let simmer for 30 minutes. Remove from heat. Pour mixture through a colander or sieve to remove vegetables. Add salt, paprika and sugar and mix well. Place mixture in refrigerator until chilled. If desired, serve tomato juice over ice.

Scrumptious Strawberry Shake

Makes 2 servings

2 C. milk
1 T. honey
1 tsp. vanilla

1 C. frozen strawberries
2 whole strawberries,
   optional

In a blender, combine milk, honey, vanilla and frozen strawberries. Blend mixture until smooth and pour into glasses or goblets to serve. If desired, garnish glasses with a strawberry placed on the rim.

Orange Glorious

Makes 3 (12 ounce) servings

1 C. milk
1 C. ice water
1 (6 oz.) can frozen orange
   juice concentrate

12 ice cubes
1/4 tsp. vanilla
1/8 C. sugar
Orange peel, optional

In a blender, combine milk, ice water, orange juice concentrate, ice cubes, vanilla and sugar. Blend mixture until smooth and pour into glasses or goblets to serve. If desired, garnish with a twist of orange peel.

Creamy Tropical Shakes

Makes 4 servings

2 oranges, peeled and
   quartered
2 bananas, peeled
2 1/2 C. red or green seedless
   grapes, divided

12 ice cubes, crushed
2 tsp. honey

In a blender, combine quartered oranges, peeled bananas and 2 cups seedless grapes. Blend until smooth then add crushed ice and honey. Blend mixture until smooth and pour into glasses or goblets to serve. Garnish with remaining 1/2 cup seedless grapes floating in glass.

Chocolate Banana Peanut Butter Shake

Makes 2 servings

2 C. milk
4 T. Carnation chocolate
    instant breakfast mix

2 T. crunchy peanut butter
2 bananas, peeled and sliced
4 ice cubes

In a blender, combine milk, instant breakfast mix, peanut butter, banana slices and ice cubes. Blend for 30 seconds or until smooth. Pour into 2 glasses and serve immediately.

Vanilla Chiller

Makes 3 servings

1 C. prepared vanilla-
    flavored coffee
4 triangles Toblerone
    chocolate, coarsely
    chopped

2 C. vanilla ice cream,
    softened
6 T. whipped topping,
    divided

In a blender, combine vanilla-flavored coffee and chopped Toblerone chocolate. Blend at high speed for 30 seconds. Add ice cream and pulse until mixture is smooth. Pour liquid into 3 tall glasses. If desired, garnish each serving with 2 tablespoons whipped topping. Serve immediately.

Amazing Bruschetta

Makes 6 servings

2 large tomatoes, coarsely
    chopped
1/2 onion, chopped
2 T. olive oil
1 T. fresh chopped oregano

1 tsp. fresh chopped basil
2 tsp. fresh chopped parsley
1/2 loaf Italian bread, sliced
1/4 C. grated Parmesan
    cheese

Preheat oven to 400°. In a medium bowl, combine chopped tomatoes, chopped onions, olive oil, chopped oregano, chopped basil and chopped parsley. Place bread slices on a baking sheet and top each slice with some of the tomato mixture. Sprinkle grated Parmesan cheese over each slice. Bake in oven for 8 to 10 minutes, until bottom of bread slices are browned. Let cool 5 minutes before serving.

Asiago Dip

Makes 2 cups

1 C. light mayonnaise
1/2 C. thinly sliced green
    onions
1/3 C. plus 1 T. grated Asiago
    or Parmesan cheese,
    divided

1/4 C. sliced mushrooms
1/4 C. sun-dried tomato
    sprinkles
1 (8 oz.) container sour cream
32 (1/2" thick) slices toasted
    French baguette or
    crackers

Preheat oven to 350°. In a medium bowl, combine mayonnaise, sliced green onions, 1/3 cup Asiago or Parmesan cheese, sliced mushrooms, sun-dried tomato sprinkles and sour cream. Mix well and transfer mixture to a 1-quart glass baking dish. Sprinkle remaining 1 tablespoon cheese over mixture. Bake in oven for 30 minutes, until bubbly. Serve with toasted baguette slices or crackers.

Baked Fruit Dip

Makes 12 servings

1 (16 oz.) pkg. cream cheese
    with pineapple, softened
3/4 lb. shredded Swiss cheese

2 C. dried cranberries
2 T. orange juice
1/4 C. apple juice

Preheat oven to 375°. In a medium bowl, combine cream cheese, Swiss cheese, dried cranberries, orange juice and apple juice. Mix well and transfer to a 9" pie pan. Bake in oven for 15 minutes, until bubbly and lightly browned. Serve as a dip for fresh cut fruits or as a spread for crackers.

Vegetarian Quesadillas

Makes 6 servings

12 (8") flour tortillas
1 (11 oz.) can Mexicali corn,
    drained
1 (15 oz.) can small red or
    black beans, drained,
    rinsed and lightly mashed

2 C. taco-flavored shredded
    cheese
1 (4 oz.) can diced green
    chilies

Preheat broiler and coat broiler pan with nonstick cooking spray. Place 6 tortillas on the prepared pan. Coat tortillas lightly with cooking spray and flip over. In a medium bowl, combine drained corn, lightly mashed red or black beans, shredded cheese and diced green chilies. Spread an even amount of mixture over each tortilla. Top with remaining 6 tortillas and coat with cooking spray. Place pan under broiler for 45 to 60 seconds on each side, until lightly browned. Turn off broiler and place pan in cooler part of oven. Let sit for 1 to 2 minutes with the oven door open. To serve, cut each quesadilla into quarters.

"The Works" Nachos

Makes 2 servings

1/3 lb. ground beef
1/2 C. chunky salsa
16 tortilla chips
2 T. shredded Monterey Jack
  or mozzarella cheese

1/4 C. chopped tomato
1 T. chopped jalapeno
  peppers

In a large nonstick skillet over medium heat, combine ground beef and salsa. Cook for 5 minutes, until ground beef is cooked throughout, stirring occasionally. Arrange tortilla chips on a plate. Top with ground beef mixture and sprinkle with shredded cheese, chopped tomatoes and chopped jalapeno peppers. Serve immediately.

Maple Praline Trail Mix

Makes 10 servings

5 1/2 C. Crispix cereal
1/2 C. chopped pecans
1/3 C. maple syrup
3 T. butter or margarine,
    melted

2 tsp. vanilla
1/4 C. shredded coconut
1 T. sesame seeds

Preheat oven to 300°. Grease a jelly roll pan and set aside. In a large bowl, combine Crispix cereal and chopped pecans. In a separate bowl, combine maple syrup, melted butter, vanilla, shredded coconut and sesame seeds. Mix well and pour over cereal mixture. Toss until evenly coated. Spread mixture in an even layer onto prepared pan. Bake in oven for 30 minutes, stirring twice during baking time. Let cool completely and store in an airtight container.

Brie & Cranberry Pizza

Makes 8 servings

1 (8 oz.) can refrigerated crescent rolls
8 oz. Brie cheese, cubed

3/4 C. cranberry sauce
1/2 C. chopped pecans

Preheat oven to 425°. Lightly grease a 12" pizza pan or 9x13" baking dish. Unroll crescent rolls and separate into triangles. Arrange triangles in pan with tips pointing toward the center. Lightly press the seams together. Bake in oven for 5 minutes, until lightly browned. Remove from oven and sprinkle with cubed Brie cheese. Spoon cranberry sauce over cheese and top with chopped pecans. Bake in oven for an additional 8 minutes or until the cheese is melted. Let cool for 5 minutes before cutting into wedges or squares.

Corn Salsa Tostadas

Makes 3 dozen

3 (8") flour tortillas
3/4 C. sour cream
2 green onions, finely
  chopped
3 tsp. fresh minced cilantro
  or parsley, divided
1/4 tsp. garlic powder

3/4 C. fresh or frozen corn,
  thawed
1 plum tomato, diced
1 T. chopped jalapeno pepper
2 T. orange juice
1 tsp. canola oil
1/2 tsp. salt

Preheat oven to 400°. To make tostadas, using a 2" round cookie cutter, cut each tortilla into 12 circles. Coat both sides of each circle with nonstick cooking spray. Place circles in a single layer on a baking sheet. Bake in oven for 4 to 5 minutes, until crispy. Remove from oven and let cool. Meanwhile, in a small bowl, combine sour cream, chopped green onions, 1 teaspoon minced cilantro and garlic powder. Cover mixture and place in refrigerator. In a separate bowl, combine corn, diced tomato, chopped jalapeno, orange juice, canola oil, salt and remaining 2 teaspoons minced cilantro. Cover and place in refrigerator. Before serving, spread 1 teaspoon sour cream mixture over each tostada. Using a slotted spoon, top each tostada with 1 teaspoon corn salsa mixture. Serve immediately.

Cheesy Breads

Makes 2 dozen slices

3 C. shredded Cheddar cheese	**1 (2 oz.) can chopped black olives, drained**
1 C. mayonnaise	**4 green onions, sliced**
1 (1 oz.) pkg. dry ranch dressing mix	**2 French baguettes, cut into 1/2" slices**

Preheat oven to 350°. In a medium bowl, combine shredded Cheddar cheese, mayonnaise, ranch dressing mix, chopped black olives and sliced green onions. If mixture seems too dry, add more mayonnaise. Spread an even amount of Cheddar cheese mixture on bread slices. Arrange slices in a single layer on greased baking sheets. Bake in oven for 15 minutes, until cheese is bubbly and lightly browned. Serve warm.

Delicious Bean Dip

Makes 6 servings

1/2 lb. uncooked Cannellini beans
1 C. extra-virgin olive oil

2 cloves garlic, minced
2 T. fresh chopped sage
Salt to taste

In a 2-quart pot, soak Cannellini beans in water overnight. In the morning, rinse and add new water to cover the beans. Place pot with beans over high heat and bring to a boil for 20 to 25 minutes, until tender. Drain pot and add olive oil. Using a potato masher, mash beans until creamy in texture. Add minced garlic and chopped sage and mix well. Season with salt to taste. Serve cold as a dip for chips.

Mexican Cream Cheese Roll-Ups

Makes 8 to 10 servings

1 (8 oz.) pkg. cream cheese,
    softened
1/3 C. mayonnaise
2/3 C. chopped green olives

1 (2 1/4 oz.) can chopped
    black olives, drained
6 green onions, chopped
8 (10") flour tortillas
1/2 C. salsa

In a medium bowl, combine cream cheese, mayonnaise, chopped green and black olives and chopped green onions. Spread mixture in a thin layer onto each tortilla. Roll up tortillas. Chill in refrigerator for about 1 hour, until filling is firm. Slice tortillas into 1" rolls. If necessary, secure rolls with toothpicks. Serve with salsa for dipping.

Breads
& Sides

Cinnamon Swirl Bread

Makes 2 loaves

1 C. milk	1 tsp. salt
2 eggs	1 1/2 tsp. active dry yeast
1/4 C. plus 2 T. butter or	1/2 C. brown sugar
margarine, softened,	1/2 C. chopped walnuts or
divided	pecans, toasted*
4 C. bread flour	2 tsp. cinnamon
1/4 C. sugar	Powdered sugar, sifted

Preheat oven to 350°. In a large bowl, combine milk, eggs, 1/4 cup butter, bread flour, sugar, salt and active dry yeast. Mix well and let dough rise. Punch down dough, cover and let rest for 10 minutes. Meanwhile, in a medium bowl, combine brown sugar, toasted nuts and cinnamon and set aside. Divide dough into 2 parts. On a lightly floured surface, roll each part into a 9x14" rectangle. Spread 1 rectangle with 1 tablespoon butter and sprinkle with half of the brown sugar mixture. Roll up the 2 short sides of the rectangle into a spiral until they meet in the middle. Repeat with remaining rectangle, remaining 1 tablespoon butter and remaining brown sugar mixture. Place loaves, rolled sides up, into two 5x9" loaf pans. Cover pans and let rise for about 30 minutes, until doubled in size. Bake in oven for about 30 minutes, until bread sounds hollow when lightly tapped. To prevent excess browning, cover loaves with aluminum foil for last 10 minutes of baking time. Remove loaves from pan and let cool on a wire rack. Before serving, sprinkle loaves with sifted powdered sugar.

* To toast, place chopped nuts in a single layer on a baking sheet. Bake at 350* for approximately 10 minutes or until nuts are golden brown.

High Protein Bread Maker Bread

Makes 1 (1 pound) loaf

1 T. canola oil	1/4 C. soy flour
1 T. honey	1/4 C. powdered soy milk
1 C. water	1/4 C. oat bran
1 C. bread flour	1 tsp. salt
1 C. whole wheat flour	2 tsp. active dry yeast

Using a bread maker, place canola oil, honey and water in the pan. In a medium bowl, combine bread flour, whole wheat flour, soy flour, powdered soy milk, oat bran and salt. Mix well and pour over liquids in pan. Do not mix. Make a well in the center of the dry ingredients and place yeast in the center, keeping yeast away from liquids. On the bread maker, select the basic medium or regular setting. Press Start.

Orange Juice Bread

Makes 1 loaf

1/2 C. sweet butter, softened
1 1/4 C. plus 1/3 C. sugar, divided
2 large eggs, beaten
1 1/2 C. flour
1 tsp. baking powder
1/4 tsp. salt

1/4 C. plus 1 T. orange juice, divided
1/4 C. milk
Zest of 1 lemon
Zest of 1 orange
1 T. lemon juice

Preheat oven to 325°. In a large bowl, cream together butter and 1 1/4 cups sugar. Add beaten eggs and mix well. Into a separate bowl, sift flour, baking powder and salt. In a separate bowl, combine 1/4 cup orange juice and milk. Alternating, add sifted dry ingredients and liquids to creamed mixture, beating well after each addition. Stir in lemon zest and orange zest. Grease a 5x9" loaf pan. Line the bottom of the pan with waxed paper and grease the waxed paper. Pour batter into prepared pan and bake in oven for 45 minutes, until a toothpick inserted in center of loaf comes out clean. To make icing, in a small saucepan over medium heat, combine remaining 1 tablespoon orange juice, lemon juice and remaining 1/3 cup sugar. Cook, stirring constantly, until sugar dissolves. Remove bread from oven and immediately spread with icing. Let bread cool in the pan.

Banana Chocolate Chip Bread

Makes 1 loaf

1 C. mashed bananas
1 C. sugar
1/4 C. canola oil
1 medium egg
1 tsp. vanilla

1/2 tsp. salt
1 tsp. baking soda
2 1/4 C. flour
1/2 C. mini chocolate chips
or nuts

Preheat oven to 325°. In a medium bowl, combine mashed bananas, sugar and oil. Mix well and add egg and vanilla. Into a large bowl, sift salt, baking soda and flour. Slowly add banana mixture to flour mixture, blending well. Add chocolate chips and mix well. Grease a 5x9" loaf pan. Pour batter into prepared pan. Bake in oven for 1 hour and 10 minutes, until a toothpick inserted in center of loaf comes out clean.

Strawberry Bread

Makes 2 loaves

2 C. fresh strawberries, sliced | 1 tsp. baking soda
2 C. plus 1 T. sugar, divided | 1 1/4 C. vegetable oil
3 1/8 C. flour | 4 eggs, beaten
1 T. cinnamon | 1 1/4 C. chopped pecans
1 tsp. salt

Preheat oven to 350°. Grease and flour two 5x9" loaf pans and set aside. In a large bowl, place sliced strawberries. Sprinkle strawberries lightly with 1 tablespoon sugar and set aside. In a large bowl, combine remaining 2 cups sugar, flour, cinnamon, salt and baking soda. Mix well. Add vegetable oil and beaten eggs to strawberries. Mix strawberry mixture into flour mixture, blending just until moistened. Stir in chopped pecans. Divide batter into prepared pans. Bake in oven for 45 to 50 minutes, until a toothpick inserted in center of loaves comes out clean. Remove from oven and let cool in pans for 10 minutes. Turn out loaves onto a wire rack.

Colonial Brown Bread

Makes 2 loaves

4 C. whole wheat flour	4 tsp. baking soda
1 1/3 C. flour	1 tsp. salt
1 C. brown sugar	4 C. buttermilk

Preheat oven to 350°. Grease two 5x9" loaf pans. In a large bowl, combine whole wheat flour, flour, brown sugar, baking soda and salt. Pour in buttermilk and mix well. Divide batter into prepared pans. Bake in oven for 1 hour, until a toothpick inserted in center of loaves comes out clean. Remove from oven and let cool in pans for 10 minutes. Turn out loaves onto a wire rack.

Pumpkin Cranberry Bread

Makes 2 loaves

3 C. flour	1 (15 oz.) can pumpkin puree
5 tsp. pumpkin pie spice	4 eggs
2 tsp. baking soda	1 C. vegetable oil
1 1/2 tsp. salt	1/2 C. orange juice
3 C. sugar	1 C. fresh or frozen cranberries

Preheat oven to 350°. Grease and flour two 5x9" loaf pans. In a large bowl, combine flour, pumpkin pie spice, baking soda and salt. In a large mixing bowl, beat sugar, pumpkin puree, eggs, vegetable oil and orange juice at low speed just until blended. Add pumpkin mixture to flour mixture and stir just until moistened. Gently fold in cranberries. Spoon batter into prepared loaf pans. Bake in oven for 60 to 65 minutes, until a toothpick inserted in center of loaves comes out clean. Remove from oven and let cool in pans for 10 minutes. Turn out loaves onto a wire rack.

Cheddar Bay Biscuits

Makes 20 biscuits

4 C. Bisquick baking mix	**1 tsp. garlic powder**
1/4 C. to 1/2 C. shredded	**1/4 tsp. salt**
Cheddar cheese	**1/8 tsp. onion powder**
1 1/3 C. water	**1/8 tsp. dried parsley**
1/2 C. butter, melted	

Preheat oven to 375°. Lightly grease a baking sheet or line with parchment paper. In a medium mixing bowl, combine Bisquick baking mix, shredded Cheddar cheese and water. Mix until dough is firm. Using a small scoop, place dough on prepared baking sheet. Bake in oven for 10 to 12 minutes, until golden brown. In a small bowl, combine melted butter, garlic powder, salt, onion powder and dried parsley. Remove biscuits from oven and immediately brush with melted butter mixture. Serve warm.

Muffins That Taste Like Donuts

Makes 1 dozen

1 3/4 C. flour	1/3 C. oil
1 1/2 tsp. baking powder	1 1/2 C. sugar, divided
1/2 tsp. salt	1 egg
1/2 tsp. nutmeg	3/4 C. milk
1 1/4 tsp. cinnamon, divided	1/2 C. butter, melted

Preheat oven to 350°. In a large bowl, combine flour, baking powder, salt, nutmeg and 1/4 teaspoon cinnamon. In a separate bowl, combine oil, 3/4 cup sugar, egg and milk. Add oil mixture to dry ingredients and mix well. Grease the cups of a standard muffin tin. Spoon batter into prepared muffin cups. Bake in oven for 20 to 25 minutes. Meanwhile, in a small bowl, combine remaining 3/4 cup sugar and remaining 1 teaspoon cinnamon. Remove muffins from oven and let cool. Once muffins have cooled, dip the tops into the melted butter and then into the sugar and cinnamon mixture. Let cool completely before serving.

⚹ Sweet Corn Muffins

Makes 1 dozen

1/4 C. butter, softened	**1 1/2 C. Bisquick baking mix**
1/2 C. plus 1 T. sugar	**1/4 C. yellow cornmeal**
2 eggs	**2/3 C. milk**
1 T. vanilla	

Preheat oven to 375°. Grease the cups of a standard muffin tin. In a large bowl, cream together butter and sugar until lightened and fluffy. Add eggs, one at a time, beating well after each addition. Mix in vanilla. In a separate bowl, combine Bisquick baking mix and cornmeal. Alternating, add cornmeal mixture and milk to butter mixture, stirring until just combined. Spoon batter into prepared muffin cups. Bake in oven for 20 to 30 minutes, until muffins are golden brown.

Blueberry Muffins

Makes 1 dozen

1 C. milk

1 egg

1/3 C. vegetable oil

2 C. flour

2 tsp. baking powder

1/2 C. sugar

1/2 C. fresh blueberries

Preheat oven to 400°. Grease or line the cups of a standard muffin tin. In a large bowl, combine milk, egg and vegetable oil. Mix well and add flour, baking powder, sugar and blueberries. Gently mix batter a few times. Spoon batter into prepared muffin cups. Bake in oven for 20 minutes. Serve warm.

Apple Streusel
Pumpkin Muffins

Makes 1 1/2 dozen

2 1/2 C. plus 2 T. flour,
   divided
2 1/4 C. sugar, divided
1 T. pumpkin pie spice
1 tsp. baking soda
1/2 tsp. salt
2 eggs, lightly beaten

1 C. canned pumpkin puree
1/2 C. vegetable oil
2 C. peeled, cored and
   chopped apples
1/2 tsp. cinnamon
1 1/2 T. butter, softened

Preheat oven to 350°. Lightly grease 18 muffin cups or line muffin cups with paper liners. Into a large bowl, sift 2 1/2 cups flour, 2 cups sugar, pumpkin pie spice, baking soda and salt. In a separate bowl, combine lightly beaten eggs, pumpkin puree and vegetable oil. Add pumpkin mixture to flour mixture, stirring just until moistened. Fold in chopped apples. Spoon batter into prepared muffin cups. In a small bowl, combine remaining 2 tablespoons flour, 1/4 cup sugar and cinnamon. Cut in butter until mixture resembles coarse crumbs. Sprinkle topping evenly over muffin batter in cups. Bake in oven for 35 to 40 minutes or until a toothpick inserted in center of muffins comes out clean. Remove from oven and cool on a wire rack.

Warm Creole Potato Salad

Makes 4 servings

4 slices bacon, diced
1 small onion, chopped
1 1/2 lbs. small new potatoes,
    scrubbed and cut
    into eighths
2 T. cider vinegar
1 1/2 T. molasses

1/2 tsp. salt
1/2 tsp. hot pepper sauce
1 1/2 T. ketchup
1 T. vegetable oil
1 stalk celery, diced
2 T. fresh chopped parsley

In a microwave-safe 9x13" baking dish, place diced bacon along the bottom. Cover with paper towels and microwave on high for 1 1/2 minutes. Uncover and stir in chopped onions. Microwave for 1 additional minute. Add cut potatoes to baking dish and cover. Microwave for 4 minutes. Stir and return to microwave for an additional 4 minutes, until potatoes are tender. Meanwhile, in a large bowl, combine cider vinegar, molasses, salt, hot pepper sauce, ketchup and vegetable oil. Add potato mixture to bowl with vinegar mixture. Toss until evenly coated. Let stand for 8 minutes. Add diced celery and chopped parsley. Toss again until evenly coated.

Mediterranean Rice Salad

Makes 4 servings

1 1/4 C. water
1/2 tsp. salt
2 C. instant brown rice
3/4 C. light Italian salad
   dressing
1 (12 oz.) can tuna, drained
   and flaked

1 (9 oz.) pkg. frozen
   French-cut green beans,
   thawed and drained
1 C. pitted small black olives
1/4 to 1/2 tsp. pepper
Large lettuce leaves
3 small tomatoes, cored
   and cut into wedges

In a medium saucepan over medium heat, combine water and salt. Bring to a boil and stir in instant brown rice. Remove from heat, cover and set aside for 10 minutes, until water is completely absorbed. Transfer rice to a large bowl. Add dressing and mix gently. Using a rubber spatula, fold in flaked tuna, green beans, olives and pepper. Serve immediately or chill in refrigerator for several hours. To serve, arrange large lettuce leaves on 4 plates. Spoon salad over lettuce leaves and garnish with tomato wedges.

Cajun Potato Wedges on the Grill

Makes 4 to 6 servings

3 large russet potatoes,
   washed and scrubbed
1/4 C. olive oil
2 cloves garlic, minced
1 tsp. paprika
1 tsp. salt

1/2 tsp. dried thyme
1/2 tsp. dried oregano
1/4 tsp. pepper
1/8 to 1/4 tsp. cayenne pepper
2 C. mesquite grilling chips

Preheat grill and cover the grate with aluminum foil. Poke small holes in the aluminum foil. Preheat oven to 425°. Cut potatoes in half lengthwise and cut each half lengthwise into 4 wedges. Place potato wedges in a large bowl. Add olive oil and minced garlic and toss until evenly coated. In a small bowl, combine paprika, salt, dried thyme, dried oregano, pepper and cayenne pepper. Sprinkle paprika mixture over potatoes and toss until evenly coated. Place potato wedges in a single layer in a shallow roasting pan, reserving remaining oil mixture in bowl. Bake in oven for 20 minutes. Remove potato wedges from oven and cover to keep warm. Meanwhile, cover mesquite chips with cold water and soak for 20 minutes. Drain mesquite chips and sprinkle over coals in grill. Place potato wedges on aluminum foil in grill. Close grill and cook potato wedges for 15 to 20 minutes, brushing with reserved oil mixture halfway through grilling time and turning once.

The Pasta Salad

Makes 7 servings

1 (8 oz.) pkg. small shell pasta
2 eggs
2 oz. cooked ham, cut into
    thin strips
1 (10 oz.) pkg. frozen English
    peas, thawed
1 C. shredded Swiss cheese

1/2 C. mayonnaise
1/4 C. sour cream
2 green onions, chopped
1 tsp. prepared mustard
1 tsp. hot pepper sauce
1 tsp. paprika

Fill a large pot with lightly salted water and bring to a boil. Add pasta and cook for 8 to 10 minutes, until pasta is al dente. Rinse with cold water, drain and set aside. Meanwhile, place eggs in a saucepan over medium heat and cover with cold water. Bring to a boil, reduce heat and let simmer for 10 to 15 minutes. Plunge eggs immediately into cold water. Let eggs cool completely, peel and slice. In a large bowl, toss together cooked pasta, egg slices, ham strips, thawed peas and shredded Swiss cheese. In a separate bowl, combine mayonnaise, sour cream, chopped green onions, mustard and hot pepper sauce. Mix until well blended. Pour 3/4 of the dressing mixture over pasta mixture and toss until evenly coated. Spread remaining dressing evenly over salad. Sprinkle with paprika, cover tightly and chill in refrigerator for 4 hours or overnight.

Almond Rice

Makes 4 servings

1 C. chicken broth	1/8 tsp. saffron
1 C. water	1/8 tsp. salt, optional
1 C. long grain white rice	Pepper to taste
2 T. slivered almonds	

In a medium saucepan over high heat, bring chicken broth and water to a boil. Stir in long grain white rice, slivered almonds, saffron and salt. Add pepper to taste and return to a boil. Immediately reduce heat to low. Cover saucepan and let simmer for 20 to 25 minutes, until rice is tender and all liquid is absorbed.

Apple Carrot Salad

Makes 4 servings

1 lb. carrots, peeled and
  shredded
2 large tart apples, peeled
  and shredded
1/2 C. raisins

2 T. lemon juice
2 T. honey
1/2 tsp. vanilla
1 C. plain yogurt

In a medium bowl, combine shredded carrots, shredded apples and raisins. In a separate bowl, whisk together lemon juice, honey, vanilla and yogurt. Pour yogurt mixture over carrot mixture. Toss until evenly coated and chill in refrigerator until ready to serve.

Mexican Pasta Salad

Makes 4 servings

1/2 lb. rotini or other spiral
    pasta
2 tomatoes, seeded and diced
1 1/2 C. frozen corn, thawed
2 carrots, peeled and
    shredded
1/4 C. red onion, chopped
1 T. Dijon mustard

1 T. lime juice
1 T. jalapeno pepper, seeded
    and minced
3/4 tsp. chili powder
3/4 tsp. ground cumin
1 C. fresh chopped cilantro
Salt and pepper to taste

Fill a large pot with lightly salted water and bring to a boil. Add pasta and cook for 8 to 10 minutes, until pasta is al dente. Rinse with cold water and drain. Add diced tomatoes, corn, shredded carrots and chopped red onions and mix well. In a jar with a tight-fitting lid, combine Dijon mustard, lime juice, minced jalapeno peppers, chili powder and ground cumin. Shake vigorously and pour dressing over pasta mixture. Add fresh chopped cilantro and toss until evenly coated. Season with salt and pepper to taste.

Easy Ranch Beans

Makes 4 servings

1/4 C. chopped green bell
   pepper
1 3/4 C. canned baked beans
1 3/4 C. canned red kidney
   beans, drained and rinsed

2 T. ketchup
2 T. molasses
1/2 tsp. onion powder

In a large saucepan over medium high heat, combine chopped green bell peppers, baked beans, rinsed red kidney beans, ketchup, molasses and onion powder. Mix well and cook about 10 minutes or until heated throughout.

Grilled Sweet Potatoes

Makes 4 servings

4 medium sweet potatoes, peeled
1/3 C. Dijon mustard
2 T. olive oil

1 T. fresh minced rosemary or 1 tsp. dried rosemary
1/2 tsp. salt
1/4 tsp. pepper

Preheat grill and cover the grate with aluminum foil. Cut sweet potatoes diagonally into 1/2" thick slices. Place potatoes in a shallow microwave-safe dish with 1 cup water. Cover with plastic wrap, puncturing the plastic wrap in several places. Microwave on high for 6 minutes, until potatoes are crispy tender, turning once. If necessary, potatoes can be cooked in 2 batches. Drain well. In a small bowl, combine Dijon mustard, olive oil, rosemary, salt and pepper. Brush mixture over potato slices on both sides. Lightly oil the aluminum foil on grill. Place sweet potato slices on aluminum foil and grill over medium high heat for 5 to 8 minutes, turning and basting often with Dijon mustard mixture, until potatoes are tender.

Best-Ever Broccoli Salad

Makes 6 servings

10 slices bacon	**3 T. white wine vinegar**
1 head broccoli,	**2 T. sugar**
cut into pieces	**1 C. mayonnaise**
1/4 C. chopped red onions	**1 C. sunflower seeds**
1/2 C. raisins	

In a large, deep skillet over medium heat, cook bacon until evenly browned and crispy. Drain skillet, crumble bacon and set aside. In a medium bowl, combine broccoli, chopped red onions and raisins. In a separate bowl, whisk together vinegar, sugar and mayonnaise. Pour vinegar mixture over broccoli mixture and toss until evenly coated. Cover and chill in refrigerator for 2 hours. Before serving, toss salad with crumbled bacon and sunflower seeds.

Orzo & Tomato Salad

Makes 6 servings

1 C. orzo pasta
1/4 C. green olives
1 C. crumbled feta cheese
3 T. fresh chopped parsley
3 T. fresh chopped dillweed

1 medium tomato, chopped
1/4 C. olive oil
1/8 C. lemon juice
Salt and pepper to taste

In a large pot of lightly salted boiling water, cook orzo for 8 to 10 minutes, until al dente. Drain pot and rinse pasta with cold water. When orzo is cooled, place in a medium bowl. Add green olives, crumbled feta cheese, chopped parsley, chopped dillweed and chopped tomatoes. In a small bowl, whisk together olive oil and lemon juice. Pour mixture over salad and mix well. Season with salt and pepper to taste. Chill in refrigerator until ready to serve.

Desserts

Glazed Jelly Doughnuts

Makes 10 doughnuts

1 (10 oz.) tube fluffy
    buttermilk biscuits
10 tsp. raspberry jelly,
    divided
2 T. sugar
1 tsp. cinnamon

1 T. butter, melted
1 C. powdered sugar
2 T. milk
1/2 tsp. vanilla
Pinch of salt

Preheat oven to 400°. Grease an 8" or 9" round pan. Separate buttermilk biscuits into 10 rounds and cut a slit in the side of each biscuit to form a deep pocket. Fill each pocket with 1 teaspoon raspberry jelly and press cut edge to firmly seal the jelly inside. Arrange biscuits in pan. In a small bowl, combine sugar and cinnamon and sprinkle mixture over biscuits in pan. Drizzle melted butter over biscuits. Bake in oven for 15 to 20 minutes, until golden. In a medium bowl, combine powdered sugar, milk, vanilla and salt, mixing until smooth. Drizzle the glaze over biscuits.

Chocolate-Walnut Tart

Makes 8 servings

1 prepared pie crust	**1/4 C. butter**
1 C. chocolate chips	**1/2 C. brown sugar**
1 C. coarsely chopped	**3/4 C. dark corn syrup**
walnuts	**3 eggs**
1 tsp. vanilla	**Whipped topping, optional**

Preheat oven to 350°. Place oven rack in lower third of oven. Fit pie crust into a 9" or 11" round tart pan. Sprinkle chocolate chips and chopped walnuts over pie crust. In a large glass bowl, melt butter in microwave. Add brown sugar, corn syrup, eggs and vanilla and beat until smooth. Pour mixture into pie crust. Bake in oven for 30 minutes for an 11" tart and 45 minutes for a 9" tart. Let cool on a wire rack before serving. If desired, serve with whipped topping.

Phyllo Pockets

Makes 8 servings

1 prepared pound cake
1/3 C. seedless raspberry
   jam, melted
1/2 pint raspberries, divided
1/2 C. butter
8 sheets frozen phyllo
   dough, thawed according
   to package directions

1 1/2 C. powdered sugar
4 (1 oz.) squares bittersweet
   baking chocolate,
   finely chopped

Preheat oven to 400°. Cut pound cake horizontally into four 1/3" thick slices. Using a cookie cutter, cut each slice into two 2 1/2" rounds. Brush melted jam over each round and top with 5 raspberries. Set aside remaining raspberries. In a small saucepan over low heat, melt butter. Place phyllo sheets on a flat surface. Cover phyllo sheets with a damp cloth. Remove 1 sheet and brush lightly and completely with melted butter. Dust with 2 tablespoons powdered sugar. Cut buttered phyllo in half crosswise and stack the 2 pieces, rotating 1 piece slightly. Place 1 pound cake in the center of the phyllo and sprinkle with 1/8 of the chopped chocolate. Fold both pieces of phyllo up and around the cake, pinching together at the top. Brush top and sides with butter. Place phyllo pocket in a freezer bag while assembling 7 more pockets in the same way. Grease a baking sheet and place phyllo pockets on baking sheet. Bake in oven for 6 to 8 minutes, until phyllo begins to brown. Remove from oven and dust lightly with remaining powdered sugar. Garnish with remaining raspberries.

Maple Baked Bananas

Makes 4 servings

2 T. butter
2 T. maple syrup
2 T. brown sugar
1 T. fresh lime juice
1/2 tsp. allspice

4 medium bananas, peeled
and halved lengthwise
2 T. shredded coconut
Vanilla ice cream or frozen
yogurt

Preheat oven to 375°. In a 9" square pan, place butter then place pan in oven to melt butter. Remove from oven and add maple syrup, brown sugar, lime juice and allspice. Arrange bananas in pan, cut side up. Sprinkle with shredded coconut. Bake in oven for 12 minutes, turning bananas over after 6 minutes. Baste bananas with liquid in pan when turning. Remove from oven and place bananas in 4 dessert bowls. Top with ice cream. Spoon sauce from baking pan over ice cream.

Orange Pecan
Angel Food Cake

Makes 12 servings

2/3 C. finely chopped pecans
2 T. sugar
1 T. light corn syrup
1 1/2 tsp. cinnamon
1 1/2 tsp. grated orange peel

1/2 tsp. orange extract
1 (18 1/4 oz.) box angel food
   cake mix
1/2 C. powdered sugar
2 tsp. milk

Preheat oven to 350°. In a medium bowl, combine chopped pecans, sugar, corn syrup, cinnamon, grated orange peel and orange extract. In a large mixing bowl, prepare cake mix batter according to package directions, beating at medium high speed. Spoon half of the batter into an ungreased 10" tube pan. Sprinkle a ring of the pecan mixture over batter, keeping mixture away from sides of pan and tube. Top with remaining batter. Bake in oven for 45 to 50 minutes or until crust is golden and cracked. Invert pan onto its legs and let cool for about 1 1/2 hours. Loosen edges of cooled cake and remove from pan. To make glaze, in a small bowl, combine powdered sugar and milk. Drizzle glaze over cooled cake.

Blackberry Jelly Roll

Makes 8 servings

4 T. powdered sugar, divided	3/4 C. sugar
1 C. flour	2 tsp. grated lemon peel
1 tsp. baking powder	1/4 C. fresh lemon juice
1/4 tsp. salt	1 tsp. vanilla
4 eggs	1 (12 oz.) jar blackberry jam

Preheat oven to 375°. Grease a jelly roll pan and line with waxed paper. Grease the waxed paper. Lay a kitchen towel on a flat surface and dust with 2 tablespoon powdered sugar. In a small bowl, whisk together flour, baking powder and salt. In a medium mixing bowl, beat eggs at medium speed about 5 minutes until thick and lemon colored. Gradually add sugar, beating until well blended. Add grated lemon peel, lemon juice and vanilla and mix well. Gently fold in flour mixture, stirring until well combined. Pour batter into prepared pan and spread evenly. Bake in oven for 12 to 15 minutes, until a toothpick inserted in center of cake comes out clean. Remove from oven and immediately invert cake onto powdered sugar dusted towel. Remove waxed paper from cake and lift up 1 side of the towel and roll towel and cake together into a log. Let cool completely on a wire rack. Unroll and remove towel. Spread blackberry jam evenly over cake. Reroll into a log and dust with remaining 2 tablespoons powdered sugar. To serve, cut jelly roll into slices.

Mocha Sour Cream Cake

Makes 12 servings

3 T. plus 1 tsp. instant
   espresso powder,
   divided
1/4 C. coffee-flavored
   liqueur or strong
   brewed coffee
1 (18 1/4 oz.) chocolate
   cake mix
4 eggs

2 C. sour cream, divided
1/3 C. canola or vegetable oil
10 (1 oz.) squares semisweet
   chocolate, chopped
1/2 tsp. cinnamon
Whipped topping, optional
Chocolate covered espresso
   beans, optional

Preheat oven to 325°. Grease two 9" round pans and set aside. In a small bowl, combine 3 tablespoons instant espresso powder and liqueur. In a large mixing bowl, combine chocolate cake mix, eggs, 1 cup sour cream, oil and espresso mixture. Beat at low speed until blended. Increase speed to medium and beat for 2 minutes. Divide batter into prepared pans. Bake in oven for 30 to 32 minutes, until a toothpick inserted in center of cake comes out clean. Remove cakes from oven and let cool completely. To make frosting, in a glass bowl, place chopped chocolate. Heat in microwave for 90 seconds or until melted, stirring often. Stir in remaining 1 cup sour cream, remaining 1 teaspoon espresso powder and cinnamon. Place 1 cake on serving plate. Spread with half of the frosting. Top with second cake. Spread remaining frosting on top of cake. If desired, garnish with whipped cream and chocolate covered espresso beans.

Pumpkin Spice Cake

Makes 12 servings

1 (18 1/4 oz.) yellow cake mix	3 eggs
2 1/2 tsp. cinnamon	1 (8 oz.) pkg. cream cheese,
3 tsp. ground ginger, divided	softened
1 C. canned pumpkin puree	1/4 C. butter, softened
1/2 C. water	1 tsp. vanilla
1/3 C. canola or vegetable oil	2 3/4 C. powdered sugar

Place oven rack at top of lower third of oven. Preheat oven to 325°. Grease a 9x13" baking pan and set aside. In a medium mixing bowl, beat together yellow cake mix, cinnamon, 2 1/2 teaspoons ground ginger, pumpkin puree, water, oil and eggs at low speed until blended. Increase speed to medium and beat for an additional 2 minutes. Scrape batter into prepared pan. Bake in oven for 35 to 40 minutes, until a toothpick inserted in center of cake comes out clean. Meanwhile, to make frosting, in a large mixing bowl, beat together cream cheese, butter and vanilla at low speed until smooth. Add remaining 1/2 teaspoon ground ginger and powdered sugar, 1 cup at a time, beating until frosting is blended and smooth. Remove cake from oven and spread frosting over top and sides of cake.

Five Minute Fudge

Makes 14 pieces

2/3 C. undiluted
   evaporated milk
2 T. butter
1 2/3 C. sugar
1 tsp. vanilla

2 C. miniature
   marshmallows
1/2 C. chopped nuts
1 1/2 C. chocolate chips

Grease an 8" or 9" square pan and set aside. In a medium saucepan, combine evaporated milk, butter and sugar. Place saucepan over medium heat and bring to a boil. Cook for 5 minutes, stirring constantly. Remove from heat and immediately add marshmallows, chopped nuts, chocolate chips and vanilla. Mix well, until marshmallows are melted. Pour mixture into prepared pan.

Note: Make sure all ingredients are measured and ready before preparing fudge. Timing and following directions are very important.

Apple Raisin Pie

Makes 6 servings

2 (20 oz.) cans apple pie filling	1/3 C. flour
1 C. raisins	1/4 C. brown sugar
1/4 tsp. nutmeg	3 T. butter, melted
1 prepared shortbread pie crust	3/4 C. chopped walnuts

Preheat oven to 375°. In a medium bowl, combine apple pie filling, raisins and nutmeg. Spoon mixture into prepared pie crust. In a separate bowl, combine flour and brown sugar. Add melted butter and stir until mixture is crumbly. Add chopped walnuts and mix well. Sprinkle mixture over ingredients in pie crust. Bake in oven for 40 minutes or until topping is golden brown.

Super Chunk Cookies

Makes 2 dozen

8 (1 oz.) squares semi-sweet
   baking chocolate
1/2 C. butter or margarine,
   softened
1/2 C. sugar
1/2 C. brown sugar
1 egg

1 tsp. vanilla
1 C. flour
1 C. quick-cooking oats
1/2 tsp. baking soda
1/2 C. chopped pecans,
   optional

Preheat oven to 375°. Cut chocolate squares in half. Cut each half into 3 chunks. In a large mixing bowl, beat together butter, sugar, brown sugar, egg and vanilla at medium speed for 1 minute. Add flour, oats and baking soda and beat at low speed until well blended. Add chocolate chunks and chopped pecans. Mix well and drop dough by tablespoonfuls 2" apart onto ungreased baking sheets. Bake in oven for 10 minutes, until lightly browned. Let cool on baking sheets before transferring to wire racks. Let cool completely before serving.

Chocolate Covered Cherries

Makes 16 servings

2 1/2 C. powdered sugar	**4 (4 oz.) jars maraschino**
1/4 C. margarine, softened	**cherries, drained**
1 T. milk	**2 C. chocolate chips**
1/2 tsp. almond extract	**2 T. shortening**

In a medium bowl, combine powdered sugar, margarine, milk and almond extract. Transfer mixture to a lightly floured flat surface. Knead mixture by hand into a large ball. Divide ball into 1" balls. Flatten each ball into a 2" circle. Wrap each cherry with 1 circle by lightly rolling in hands, leaving the stems sticking out. Place wrapped cherries on waxed paper and chill in refrigerator for at least 4 hours. In a medium saucepan over medium heat, melt chocolate chips and shortening and mix well. Hold 1 wrapped chilled cherry by the stem and dip into the melted chocolate mixture. Place covered cherry on waxed paper. Repeat with remaining cherries. Chill chocolate covered cherries in refrigerator until ready to serve.

The Best Brownies

Makes 1 dozen

1/2 C. flour	1 C. sugar
1/3 C. cocoa powder	1 tsp. vanilla
1/4 tsp. baking powder	2 eggs
1/4 tsp. salt	1/2 to 3/4 C. chopped
1/2 C. oil	pecans or walnuts

Preheat oven to 350°. Grease an 8" square pan and set aside. In a medium bowl, whisk together flour, cocoa powder, baking powder and salt. In a separate bowl, combine oil, sugar and vanilla. Mix well and add eggs, whisking until lightened in texture. Add flour mixture and chopped nuts and mix well. Pour mixture into prepared pan. Bake in oven for 17 to 22 minutes, until brownies pull away from sides of pan, being careful not to overbake. Serve warm or cooled.

Peach Pie

Makes 8 servings

1/3 C. flour

1 C. sugar

1/4 C. butter, softened

1 (9") double crust pie pastry

10 fresh peaches, sliced

Preheat oven to 350°. In a medium bowl, combine flour and sugar. Cut in butter until mixture resembles small crumbs. Place one pie pastry crust in the bottom of a greased 9" pie pan. Line the crust with some of the sliced peaches. Sprinkle some of the butter mixture over the peaches. Top with more peaches and crumb mixture, layer until both peaches and crumbs are used. Top peaches with remaining pie pastry crust, or cut remaining pastry into lattice strips and place over pie crust. Bake in oven for 45 minutes, until crust is golden brown. Let pie cool before cutting into pieces.

Peanut Butter Coo

Makes 3 dozen

1 (18 1/4 oz.) pkg. yellow   1/2 C. vegetab
   cake mix   2 eggs
1 C. creamy peanut butter   2 T. water

    Preheat oven to 350°. In a large bowl, pour yellow cake mix. Form a well in the center of the cake mix. Add peanut butter, vegetable oil, eggs and water to well. Mix until evenly blended. Drop dough by teaspoonfuls onto an ungreased baking sheet. Flatten cookies slightly with a fork dipped in water. Bake in oven for 10 to 12 minutes. Remove from oven and let cookies sit on baking sheet for 2 to 3 minutes before removing to a wire rack to cool.

Snickerdoodles

Makes 4 dozen

1/2 C. butter, softened	2 3/4 C. flour
1/2 C. shortening	2 tsp. cream of tartar
1 1/2 C. plus 2 T. sugar, divided	1 tsp. baking soda
	1/4 tsp. salt
2 eggs	2 tsp. cinnamon
2 tsp. vanilla	

Preheat oven to 400°. In a medium bowl, combine butter, shortening, 1 1/2 cups sugar, eggs and vanilla. Mix well and add flour, cream of tartar, baking soda, salt and cinnamon. Mix until evenly blended. Shape rounded teaspoonfuls of dough into balls. In a small bowl, combine remaining 2 tablespoons sugar and cinnamon. Roll dough balls in sugar and cinnamon mixture and place 2" apart onto ungreased baking sheets. Bake in oven for 8 to 10 minutes or until cookies are set, being careful not to overbake. Remove from oven and place immediately onto wire racks to cool.

Babe Ruth Bars

Makes 18 bars

1 C. peanut butter
1 C. corn syrup
1/2 C. brown sugar
1/2 C. sugar

6 C. cornflakes cereal
1 C. chocolate chips
2/3 C. peanuts

In a large saucepan over medium heat, combine peanut butter, corn syrup, brown sugar and sugar. Cook, stirring occasionally, until mixture is smooth. Remove from heat and immediately stir in cornflakes, chocolate chips and peanuts. Mix well until evenly coated. Press mixture into a greased 9x13" baking dish. Let cool completely before cutting into bars.

Baked Fresh Cherry Pie

Makes 8 servings

1 (9") double crust pie pastry	4 C. pitted cherries
4 T. quick-cooking tapioca	1/4 tsp. almond extract
1/8 tsp. salt	1/2 tsp. vanilla
1 C. sugar	1 1/2 T. butter

Preheat oven to 400°. Place one pie pastry crust in the bottom of a greased 9" pie pan. In a large bowl, combine tapioca, salt, sugar, cherries, almond extract and vanilla. Let stand 15 minutes. Transfer mixture to pie pan and dot with butter. Cover with top crust. Seal the edges and cut vents in the top crust. Place pie on a foil lined baking sheet in case of dripping. Bake in oven for 50 minutes or until golden brown.

Chocolate Cookie Pizza

Makes 12 to 16 slices

1/2 C. plus 2 T. butter, softened, divided	6 oz. chocolate chips
1/2 C. brown sugar	3 T. milk
1/4 C. sugar	1 C. powdered sugar
1 tsp. vanilla	1/2 C. pecan halves
1 egg	1/2 C. M&M's
1 1/4 C. flour	1/4 C. shredded coconut
1/2 tsp. baking soda	2 oz. white chocolate, melted

Preheat oven to 350°. In a large bowl, combine 1/2 cup butter, brown sugar, sugar, vanilla and egg until well combined. Add flour and baking soda to make a stiff dough. Pat dough onto an ungreased 12" pizza pan or baking sheet. Bake in oven for 15 minutes or until golden brown. Remove cookie from oven and let cool. In a saucepan over very low heat, combine chocolate chips, remaining 2 tablespoons butter and milk. Heat, stirring frequently, until chocolate is melted. Remove chocolate mixture from heat and stir in powdered sugar. Beat until smooth. If frosting is not glossy, stir in a few drops of hot water. Spread frosting over baked and cooled cookie. Immediately decorate with pecan halves, M&M's and coconut. Press toppings lightly into frosting. Drizzle melted white chocolate over toppings. Let stand until set. If desired, remove from pan and cut into wedges.

Chocolate Peanut Butter Pie

2 (4 oz.) pkgs. single serving chocolate pudding
1/3 C. creamy peanut butter

1 (8 oz.) container frozen whipped topping, thawed
1 (9") prepared graham cracker crust

In a large mixing bowl, combine chocolate pudding and peanut butter, stirring until smooth. Fold in whipped topping, stirring until evenly blended. Pour filling into prepared pie crust. Place pie in freezer until firm. Partially thaw in refrigerator for 2 hours before serving. Store leftovers in refrigerator or freezer.

Banana Split Ice Cream Pie

Makes 8 servings

2 bananas, sliced
1 (9") prepared Oreo pie crust
1 qt. strawberry ice cream,
   softened
1 (20 oz.) can crushed
   pineapple, drained

1 C. whipped topping
1/4 C. chopped walnuts
1/4 C. maraschino cherries,
   optional

Arrange sliced bananas over bottom of prepared Oreo pie crust. Spread softened strawberry ice cream over bananas. Top with drained pineapple. Spread whipped topping over pineapple and top with chopped walnuts. Place in freezer for 4 hours or until firm. If desired, garnish with maraschino cherries.

Rice Surprise

Makes 4 servings

1/3 C. white rice
1 1/2 C. heavy cream

1/3 C. sugar
**1 C. crushed pineapple,
drained**

Fill a large saucepan with lightly salted water. Bring to a boil and add rice. Reduce heat, cover and let simmer for 20 minutes. Rinse rice under cool water and place in refrigerator to chill. In a medium mixing bowl, beat heavy cream until soft peaks form, adding sugar gradually while beating. Fold drained pineapple and cooked chilled rice into whipped cream. Spoon mixture into dessert dishes and serve immediately.

Brownie Biscotti

Makes 2 1/2 dozen

1/3 C. butter, softened	2 tsp. baking powder
2/3 C. sugar	1/2 C. miniature chocolate
2 eggs	chips
1 tsp. vanilla	1 egg yolk, beaten
1 3/4 C. flour	1 T. water
1/3 C. cocoa powder	

Preheat oven to 375°. In a large bowl, cream together butter and sugar until smooth. Beat in eggs, one at a time, and stir in vanilla. In a medium bowl, combine flour, cocoa powder and baking powder. Add dry ingredients to butter mixture, stirring until well blended. Dough should be stiff. Mix in chocolate chips and chopped walnuts by hand. Divide dough into 2 equal parts. Shape dough into 2x9" loaves. Place loaves, 4" apart, on greased baking sheets. In a small bowl, combine beaten egg yolk and water. Brush egg yolk mixture over loaves. Bake in oven for 20 to 25 minutes or until loaves are firm. Remove from oven and cool on baking sheets for 30 minutes. Using a serrated knife, slice loaves diagonally into 1" slices. Return slices to baking sheet, placing slices on their side. Bake in oven for 10 to 15 minutes on each side or until dry. Cool completely and store in an airtight container.

Caramel Popcorn

Makes 20 servings

5 qts. popped popcorn	1 tsp. salt
1 C. butter	1/2 tsp. baking soda
2 C. brown sugar	1 tsp. vanilla
1/2 C. corn syrup	

Preheat oven to 250°. In a very large bowl, place popped popcorn. In a medium saucepan over medium heat, melt butter. Stir in brown sugar, corn syrup and salt. Bring to a boil, stirring constantly. Let boil for 4 minutes without stirring. Remove from heat and stir in baking soda and vanilla. Pour mixture in a thin stream over popcorn. Mix until evenly coated. Place popcorn in 2 large shallow baking dishes and bake in oven for 1 hour, stirring every 15 minutes. Remove from oven and let cool completely before breaking into pieces.

Almond Joy Cake

Makes 24 servings

1 (18 1/4 oz.) pkg. devils
   food cake mix
1 (12 oz.) can evaporated
   milk, divided
2 1/2 C. sugar, divided
25 large marshmallows

1 (14 oz.) pkg. shredded
   coconut
1/2 C. butter
2 C. chocolate chips
1 C. sliced almonds, toasted

Prepare cake mix according to package directions in a greased 9x13" baking dish. In a medium saucepan over medium high heat, combine half of the evaporated milk and 1 1/2 cups sugar. Bring to a rapid boil. Remove from heat and immediately add marshmallows. Stir until marshmallows are melted and add shredded coconut. Pour mixture over cake. In a separate saucepan over medium heat, combine remaining half of the evaporated milk and remaining 1 cup sugar. Bring to a boil and remove from heat. Add butter and chocolate chips, stirring until melted. Mix in toasted almonds. Pour mixture over coconut mixture on cake. Chill in refrigerator for at least 2 hours before serving.

Raspberry Cup Cakes

Makes 12 servings

3/4 C. graham cracker
   crumbs
1/4 C. chopped pecans
3 T. butter, melted
3/4 C. fresh raspberries,
   crushed

1/2 (8 oz.) pkg. cream
   cheese, softened
1 (10 1/2 oz.) can sweetened
   condensed milk
1 C. whipped topping

Line 12 standard muffin cups with paper liners. In a medium bowl, combine graham cracker crumbs, chopped pecans and melted butter, mixing until blended. Spoon mixture evenly into prepared muffin cups. Press down on mixture to create a firm bottom. In a blender, puree raspberries until smooth. In a medium mixing bowl, beat cream cheese at medium speed until fluffy. Add sweetened condensed milk and 1/2 cup pureed raspberries, mixing until well blended. Fold in whipped topping. Spoon mixture evenly into muffin cups. Freeze for at least 5 hours. When ready to serve, remove paper liners. Invert cup cakes onto individual serving plates. Drizzle with remaining raspberry puree. Serve immediately.

Hot Fudge Ice Cream Bar Dessert

Makes 18 servings

1 (16 oz.) can chocolate
    syrup
3/4 C. peanut butter
19 ice cream sandwiches

1 (12 oz.) container frozen
    whipped topping,
    thawed
1 C. salted peanuts

In a medium microwave-safe bowl, place chocolate syrup. Microwave on high for 2 minutes, being careful not to boil. Stir in peanut butter, mixing until smooth. Let mixture cool to room temperature. Line the bottom of a 9x13" baking dish with ice cream sandwiches. If necessary, ice cream sandwiches may be cut to fit. Spread half of the whipped topping over sandwiches. Spoon half of the chocolate mixture over whipped topping. Top with half of the salted peanuts. Repeat layers with remaining whipped topping, chocolate mixture and salted peanuts. Freeze for 1 hour or until firm. Cut into squares to serve.

Main Dishes & Soups

Southwestern Chicken Potpies

Makes 8 servings

1 T. vegetable oil
1 medium onion, diced
1 1/2 lbs. shredded cooked
   chicken
1 T. chili powder
3/4 tsp. salt
1/2 tsp. pepper
1 (13 3/4 oz.) can chicken
   broth

3 T. flour
1 (10 oz.) can Mexicali corn
1 (4 1/2 oz.) can chopped
   green chilies
1 large tomato, diced
1 tube refrigerated corn
   biscuits

Preheat oven to 350°. In a large skillet over medium high heat, heat vegetable oil. Add diced onions and cook 4 minutes, until softened. Add cooked chicken, chili powder, salt and pepper and cook for 5 minutes. In a medium bowl, whisk together chicken broth and flour. Stir mixture into skillet along with corn and chopped green chilies. Cook for 5 minutes, remove from heat and stir in diced tomatoes. Transfer mixture to 8 individual disposable foil tart pans or eight 1 1/2 cup ramekins. Divide corn biscuits into individual biscuits and roll out slightly. Place 1 biscuit over chicken mixture in each foil pan or ramekin. Cut an X in each biscuit. Bake in oven for 15 minutes, until top is browned and filling is bubbly.

Sausage Potato Casserole

3 large potatoes, peeled
and sliced thin
Pepper to taste
1 C. shredded Cheddar
cheese, divided

1 lb. Polish kielbasa
1/2 tsp. dried dillweed
1/4 tsp. caraway seeds
2/3 C. milk

Preheat oven to 375°. Line a 9x13" baking dish with aluminum foil, allowing extra foil to hang over edges of dish. Arrange sliced potatoes across bottom of baking dish. Sprinkle with pepper to taste. Top with 1/2 cup shredded Cheddar cheese. Cut kielbasa sausage in half crosswise and cut halves lengthwise. Place kielbasa, cut side down, over cheese. Top with remaining 1/2 cup shredded Cheddar cheese. Sprinkle with dried dillweed and caraway seeds. Carefully pour milk over casserole. Seal overlapping edges of aluminum up and over casserole. Bake in oven for 1 hour.

Tortilla Chicken Pie

Makes 4 servings

4 (8") flour tortillas	1 C. salsa
1 (16 oz.) can refried beans	2 C. shredded cooked
1 C. shredded Monterey	chicken
Jack cheese	

Preheat broiler. Grease a 10" microwave-safe pie pan. Place 1 tortilla in prepared pan. Spread tortilla with 1/3 of the refried beans, 1/3 of the shredded Monterey Jack cheese, 1/3 of the salsa and 1/3 of the shredded cooked chicken. Top with another tortilla and repeat layers. Top with a third tortilla and repeat layers. Top with final tortilla. Cover pan with plastic wrap and microwave on high for 8 minutes. Uncover pie and place under broiler for 30 seconds. To serve, cut chicken pie into wedges.

Pasta Romanesco

Makes 6 servings

1 lb. bowtie pasta or penne
1 (7 oz.) jar roasted red
    peppers, drained
1 (14 1/2 oz.) can chunky
    pasta-style tomatoes

1 (8 oz.) pkg. cubed
    mozzarella cheese
3 T. grated Parmesan cheese

    In a large pot of lightly salted boiling water, cook pasta until tender but firm. Drain well. To prepare sauce, in a blender or food processor, place roasted red peppers. Blend well and transfer to a serving bowl. Add tomatoes, mozzarella cheese and grated Parmesan cheese to bowl. Add drained pasta and toss until evenly coated. If desired, garnish with additional grated Parmesan cheese.

Skillet Chicken & Yellow Rice

Makes 4 servings

1 T. olive oil
1 sweet green pepper,
   cored, seeded and diced
1 C. frozen chopped onion
1 (5 oz.) pkg. yellow rice mix
1 (14 1/2 oz.) can diced
   Mexican-style tomatoes,
   drained
1 1/4 C. water
3/4 lb. chicken tenders

1/4 tsp. salt
1 C. canned pinto beans,
   drained and rinsed
1/4 C. sliced pimento-stuffed
   green olives
1/4 tsp. liquid hot pepper
   sauce
1/4 C. fresh chopped
   cilantro, optional

In a large nonstick skillet over medium heat, heat olive oil. Add diced green peppers and chopped onions. Cook for 4 minutes, stirring frequently, until softened. Add yellow rice mix, drained tomatoes and water. Cover and let simmer for 10 minutes. Sprinkle chicken tenders with salt. Stir chicken, pinto beans, sliced olives and hot pepper sauce into rice mixture. Cover and cook for 8 to 10 minutes, until rice is tender and chicken is cooked throughout. If desired, sprinkle with fresh chopped cilantro.

Turkey Jambalaya

Makes 6 servings

1 1/2 lbs. turkey sausage
3 stalks celery, chopped
1 onion, diced
1 green bell pepper, diced
3 cloves garlic, pressed

1 (14 1/2 oz.) can diced
  tomatoes in juice
2 C. chicken broth
1 1/2 C. long-grain white rice
1 bay leaf
2 tsp. Cajun seasoning

In a large skillet over medium heat, cook turkey sausage until cooked throughout. Drain skillet and set sausage aside to cool. When cooled, cut sausage into small pieces. In same skillet over medium high heat, combine chopped celery, diced onions, diced green bell peppers, pressed garlic, tomatoes in juice, chicken broth, rice, bay leaf and Cajun seasoning. Mix well and bring to a boil. Reduce heat to medium low and add sausage pieces. Cover and let simmer about 40 to 45 minutes, until rice is tender.

Teriyaki Chicken

Makes 4 servings

3/4 C. roasted-garlic teriyaki sauce
3 T. honey
4 boneless, skinless chicken breast halves

1 (8 oz.) pkg. soba noodles or vermicelli
2 green onions, chopped

In a medium bowl, combine teriyaki sauce and honey. Add chicken, making sure to cover with teriyaki mixture. Cover and refrigerate 3 hours or overnight. Preheat broiler. Coat broiler pan with nonstick cooking spray and place 6" from the heat. Partially cut chicken breast halves and spread open. Place chicken breast halves on broiler pan and, if desired, brush with additional teriyaki sauce. Broil for 4 to 5 minutes on one side. Turn chicken over, brush with more sauce and broil an additional 4 to 5 minutes, until internal temperature of chicken reaches 170°. In a small saucepan over medium heat, bring remaining marinade to a boil, until reduced by a third. Meanwhile, in a large pot of lightly salted boiling water, cook noodles about 8 minutes, until al dente. Drain well and toss with remaining reduced marinade. Slice chicken and serve over noodles. Sprinkle with chopped scallions.

Down Home Macaroni & Cheese

Makes 6 servings

4 T. butter or margarine, divided	2 C. shredded Cheddar cheese, divided
1/4 C. flour	2 C. elbow macaroni, cooked and drained
1 tsp. salt	
2 C. milk	2 T. seasoned dry bread crumbs
1/4 lb. Velveeta cheese, cubed	

Preheat oven to 350°. In a large saucepan over low heat, melt 3 tablespoons butter. Add flour and salt and cook for 1 minute, stirring frequently. Gradually add milk and cook until thickened, stirring constantly. Add cubed Velveeta cheese and 1 1/2 cups shredded Cheddar cheese and stir until cheeses are melted. Stir in cooked macaroni and pour mixture into a greased 1 1/2 quart casserole dish. In a small bowl, melt remaining 1 tablespoon butter in microwave. Toss dry bread crumbs with melted butter. Sprinkle remaining 1/2 cup shredded Cheddar cheese and bread crumb mixture over casserole. Bake in oven for 20 minutes, until heated throughout.

Five-Spice Chicken

Makes 4 servings

1 1/4 lbs. red new potatoes,
    quartered
1/2 lb. green beans, trimmed
1 medium tomato, chopped
1 T. plus 2 tsp. olive oil,
    divided
1 tsp. dried oregano

1 1/4 tsp. salt, divided
1/2 tsp. pepper
1 T. Chinese five-spice
    powder
4 boneless, skinless
    chicken breast halves

Preheat broiler. Coat broiler pan with nonstick cooking spray and place 4" from the heat. In a large pot of boiling water, cook quartered potatoes for 15 minutes, until almost tender. Add green beans to pot and cook for 5 minutes, until tender. Drain pot and transfer potatoes and green beans to a large bowl. Add tomatoes, 1 tablespoon olive oil, oregano, 3/4 teaspoon salt and pepper. Mix until evenly coated. In a small bowl, combine Chinese five-spice, remaining 2 teaspoons olive oil and remaining 1/2 teaspoon salt. Rub mixture over chicken breast halves. Place chicken on prepared pan. Place pan under broiler for 6 minutes or until internal temperature of chicken reaches 170°, turning once. Serve chicken with potato and bean salad.

Spinach Calzones
with Blue Cheese

Makes 4 servings

1 (10 oz.) can refrigerated
    pizza crust
4 cloves garlic, minced
4 C. fresh spinach leaves

8 slices Vidalia or sweet
    onion
1 1/3 C. sliced Crimini
    mushrooms
9 T. crumbled blue cheese

Preheat oven to 425°. Grease a 10 or 12" baking sheet. Unroll pizza crust and place on prepared baking sheet. Cut crust into 4 quarters. Pat each quarter into a 6x5" rectangle. Sprinkle minced garlic evenly over rectangles. Place 1 cup spinach leaves, 2 onion slices, 1/3 cup sliced mushrooms and 3 tablespoons crumbled blue cheese on each rectangle. Bring together 2 opposite corners of the rectangle, pinching at the points to seal. Bring remaining 2 corners together, pinching all points to seal. Bake in oven for 12 minutes, until calzones are golden brown.

Penne with Tomato & Bacon

Makes 6 servings

1 1/4 C. chopped onions	1/2 tsp. pepper
4 slices bacon, diced	1 lb. penne or rigatoni pasta
1 (35 oz.) can crushed tomatoes	

In a large nonstick skillet over medium high heat, sauté chopped onions and diced bacon about 5 minutes, until onions are softened. Pour drippings from skillet and discard. Stir tomatoes into skillet and cook for 8 to 10 minutes, stirring occasionally, until sauce is slightly thickened. Add pepper during last 5 minutes of cooking time. Meanwhile, in a large pot of lightly salted boiling water, cook pasta until tender but firm. Drain well. In a large serving bowl, toss together pasta and sauce.

Spaghetti with No-Cook Tomato Sauce

Makes 6 servings

1 lb. spaghetti	2 T. olive oil
2 lbs. tomatoes, diced	2 T. grated Parmesan cheese
1/2 C. shredded mozzarella cheese	3/4 tsp. salt
2 C. fresh chopped basil	1/2 tsp. pepper

In a large pot of lightly salted boiling water, cook spaghetti until tender but firm. Drain spaghetti, reserving 1/2 cup cooking water. In a large bowl, combine diced tomatoes, mozzarella, fresh chopped basil, olive oil, grated Parmesan, salt and pepper. Mix well and add cooked spaghetti and reserved cooking water. Toss until evenly coated.

Creamy Fettuccine

Makes 6 servings

1 lb. fettuccine	1/2 C. chicken broth
2 T. flour	2 C. frozen peas, thawed
3/4 tsp. salt	1/2 C. diced Canadian bacon
1/4 tsp. pepper	3 T. grated Parmesan cheese
1/4 tsp. nutmeg	1/2 C. fresh chopped basil
2 C. skim milk	

In a large pot of lightly salted boiling water, cook fettuccine until tender but firm. Drain well. Meanwhile, in a large saucepan over medium high heat, combine flour, salt, pepper and nutmeg. Whisk in milk and chicken broth and cook about 6 minutes, stirring constantly, until mixture boils and thickens. Stir in cooked fettuccine, peas, diced bacon, grated Parmesan cheese and chopped basil. Cook until heated throughout.

Tortellini with Creamy Marinara Sauce

Makes 6 servings

1 lb. cheese-filled tortellini
3 T. vodka
1/2 C. heavy cream

1 C. prepared marinara sauce
1/4 C. grated Parmesan
cheese, divided

In a large pot of lightly salted boiling water, cook tortellini until tender but firm. Drain well. Meanwhile, in a large skillet over medium heat, combine vodka and heavy cream. Bring to a boil, reduce heat and let simmer for 5 minutes, until mixture has reduced by about half. Stir in marinara sauce and bring to a simmer. Toss cooked tortellini with sauce mixture and half of the grated Parmesan cheese. Transfer to a serving dish and top with remaining half of the grated cheese.

Shells & Chicken with Olive Sauce

Makes 4 servings

3/4 lb. medium pasta shells
2 T. olive oil
1 large onion, chopped
1/2 lb. boneless, skinless
  chicken breast halves,
  cut into 1" cubes
12 large black olives,
  pitted and coarsely
  chopped

12 large green olives,
  pitted and coarsely
  chopped
1 C. fresh or canned
  diced tomatoes
3 T. fresh chopped basil
1/4 tsp. salt
1/8 tsp. pepper
Grated Parmesan cheese,
  optional

In a large pot of lightly salted boiling water, cook pasta shells until tender but firm. Drain well, reserving 1 cup cooking water. Meanwhile, in a large heavy skillet over medium high heat, heat olive oil. Add chopped onions and cook for about 2 minutes, stirring occasionally, until softened. Add chicken to skillet and heat until chicken pieces are cooked throughout. Add black and green olives, diced tomatoes and chopped basil. Bring to a boil. Add reserved 1 cup cooking water to skillet, stirring well. Return sauce to a boil over medium high heat, stirring often. Add salt and pepper, mixing until well blended. In a large serving bowl, toss shells with sauce until evenly coated. If desired, sprinkle pasta with grated Parmesan cheese.

Baked Fish

Makes 4 servings

1/4 C. butter
1/4 C. water
1/4 C. dry white wine
3 T. fresh lemon juice
1/2 tsp. salt, divided
1/4 tsp. pepper
8 large basil leaves, shredded
1 1/3 C. instant white rice
1 medium red onion,
   sliced thin
1 small sweet red pepper, cored,
   seeded and thinly sliced

1 C. frozen peas
4 flounder, haddock
   or sole filets
1/4 tsp. lemon pepper
   seasoning
1 plum tomato, sliced thin
1 loaf semolina bread
   or any kind
Lemon wedges for garnish,
   optional

Preheat oven to 450°. In a small saucepan over medium heat, combine butter, water, wine, lemon juice, 1/4 teaspoon salt, pepper and basil. Heat until butter is melted. Lay 4 squares of aluminum foil on a flat surface. Spread 1/3 cup rice in the center of each piece of aluminum foil. Top with equal amounts of onions, red pepper slices and peas. Sprinkle vegetables with remaining 1/4 teaspoon salt. Top each bundle of vegetables and rice completely with a filet. Sprinkle each filet with lemon pepper seasoning and top with tomato slices. Slightly curl up edges of foil. Divide melted butter mixture evenly among packets. Fold together 2 opposite edges of foil and fold ends up and over to completely seal each packet. Place packets on a baking sheet. Bake in oven for 20 to 25 minutes. Warm bread in oven during last few minutes of baking time. Carefully open packet, avoiding steam. Serve with warm bread slices and garnish with lemon wedges, if desired.

Clam Pizza

Makes 4 servings

2 T. garlic flavored olive oil	**1 prepared pizza shell**
2 (6 1/2 oz.) cans chopped	**1/3 C. crumbled ricotta cheese**
clams, drained	**1 C. shredded mozzarella**
	cheese

Preheat oven to 400°. In a medium skillet over low heat, heat olive oil. Add drained clams and cook for 2 minutes. Spread clam mixture evenly over pizza shell. Sprinkle ricotta and shredded mozzarella cheese evenly over pizza shell. Place pizza on a baking sheet and bake in oven for 20 minutes. Cut into 8 slices to serve.

Chicken Cheese Steaks

Makes 4 servings

1 large sweet red pepper,
  cored, seeded and cut
  lengthwise into strips
1 medium onion, cut into
  1/4" thick slices
1/2 C. bottled Caesar dressing,
  divided

4 boneless, skinless chicken
  breast halves
1 C. shredded mozzarella
  cheese
4 torpedo rolls, split in half

Preheat grill. Place aluminum foil over grate and brush aluminum foil with vegetable oil and position grate 3 to 4 inches from the heat. In a small bowl, toss red pepper and onion slices with 2 tablespoons Caesar dressing. Coat chicken breast halves with 2 tablespoons Caesar dressing. Place chicken breast halves between two sheets of plastic wrap and lightly pound to 1/4" thickness. Leave plastic wrap around chicken and place in refrigerator. Grill red pepper and onion slices on aluminum foil over grate for about 3 to 4 minutes, until tender and browned. Coarsely chop red pepper strips and onion slices and toss with remaining 4 tablespoons Caesar dressing. Remove aluminum foil from grate. Remove plastic wrap from chicken and grill for 3 minutes per side, until internal temperature of chicken reaches 170°. Place 1/4 cup shredded mozzarella cheese on each chicken breast and continue grilling until cheese is melted. Place 1 chicken breast half on each torpedo roll and top with vegetable mixture.

Shrimp Wraps

Makes 8 servings

1 (5 oz.) pkg. yellow rice mix
1 T. olive oil
1 C. chopped onions
1 C. diced sweet red peppers
2 cloves garlic, finely chopped
1 T. tomato paste
3 T. lemon juice
3/4 C. water
1/2 tsp. dried thyme
1/8 tsp. cayenne pepper

1 medium zucchini, sliced
1 large tomato, peeled,
   seeded and diced
3/4 lb. medium shrimp,
   peeled and deveined
8 (8") red pepper-flavored
   flour tortillas
Chopped tomatoes for
   garnish, optional

Prepare rice according to package directions, without adding any oil or butter. Meanwhile, in a large nonstick skillet over medium heat, heat olive oil. Add chopped onions and diced red peppers and sauté about 8 minutes, until tender. Add chopped garlic and sauté for an additional minute. Stir in tomato paste, lemon juice, water, dried thyme and cayenne pepper, cooking for about 3 minutes. Add sliced zucchini and cook, covered, for 5 minutes. Add a little water if mixture becomes too dry. Stir in diced tomatoes and shrimp. Cover and simmer for 10 minutes or until shrimp are cooked throughout. Remove from heat. Warm tortillas in microwave or oven. Spoon about 1/3 cup rice and 1/2 cup shrimp mixture in the center of each tortilla. Roll up tortillas and place, seam side down, on a serving dish. If desired, garnish with chopped tomatoes.

Beef Enchiladas

Makes 6 servings

3/4 lb. lean ground beef
1 medium onion, chopped
1 clove garlic, finely chopped
1 (4 oz.) can chopped
    green chilies
2 T. chili powder
3/4 tsp. salt
1/4 C. water
12 (6") corn tortillas

1 1/2 C. refried beans
1 C. Picante sauce
1/4 C. shredded Cheddar
    cheese
2 T. sour cream
1 medium tomato, diced
Fresh chopped cilantro for
    garnish, optional

Preheat oven to 400°. In a large nonstick skillet over medium high heat, sauté ground beef, chopped onions and chopped garlic for 3 to 4 minutes, until beef is cooked throughout. Stir in chopped chilies, chili powder, salt and water. Bring to a boil. Cook for about 10 minutes, stirring occasionally. Remove from heat. Warm tortillas in microwave or oven. Spread 2 tablespoons refried beans over each tortilla. Fill each tortilla with about 1/4 cup of the meat mixture. Roll up tortillas and place, seam side down, in a 9x13" baking dish. Repeat with remaining tortillas and lay them side by side in the baking dish. Spread Picante sauce over enchiladas and sprinkle with shredded Cheddar cheese. Bake in oven for 15 to 20 minutes, until cheese is melted and filling is hot. Top each enchilada with 1 teaspoon sour cream and diced tomatoes. If desired, garnish with chopped cilantro.

Tex-Mex Pizza

Makes 4 servings

1 (15 oz.) can black beans,
    drained and rinsed
1 (14 3/4 oz.) can salsa-style
    tomatoes, drained

1 (12") prepared thin-crust
    pizza shell
1 C. shredded Monterey
    Jack cheese
4 green onions, chopped

Preheat oven to 425°. In a medium saucepan over medium heat, cook rinsed black beans and drained tomatoes for 5 minutes, until heated throughout. Sprinkle pizza crust with 1/2 cup of the shredded Monterey Jack cheese. Sprinkle chopped green onions over cheese and spoon heated bean mixture over pizza, until entirely covered. Sprinkle remaining 1/2 cup shredded cheese over bean mixture. Bake in oven for 8 minutes, until pizza is heated throughout.

Mixed Mushroom and Tarragon Risotto

Makes 2 servings

3 C. chicken broth
1 C. white wine
2 T. butter, divided
2 C. sliced mixed mushrooms,
  such as shiitake,
  Portobello and button

1 C. thin sliced leek
1 C. Arborio rice
1/4 tsp. pepper
1 T. fresh chopped tarragon
1/4 C. grated Parmesan
  cheese

In a medium saucepan over medium heat, bring chicken broth and white wine to a simmer. In a large saucepan over medium heat, melt 1 tablespoon butter. Add sliced mushrooms to the butter and cook 3 to 5 minutes, stirring frequently, until softened. Remove mushrooms with a slotted spoon and set aside. Add remaining 1 tablespoon butter and sliced leeks to butter. Cook until leeks are softened, stirring frequently. Add rice and pepper and continue cooking for about 1 minute, until rice is thoroughly coated. Set aside 1/2 cup of the simmering broth mixture. Add remaining broth mixture to rice mixture. Reduce heat to medium low and cook for 18 to 20 minutes, stirring frequently, until rice has absorbed most of the liquid. Add chopped tarragon and mushrooms. Cook for an additional 2 minutes, stirring constantly. Add grated Parmesan cheese, stirring just to blend. If necessary, add reserved 1/2 cup broth mixture for a creamier consistency.

Spaghetti with Fresh Tomato & Butter Sauce

Makes 4 servings

2 lbs. tomatoes, peeled,
    seeded and coarsely
    chopped
6 T. butter
4 cloves garlic, lightly
    crushed

1/2 tsp. salt
3/4 lb. spaghetti
3 T. grated Parmesan cheese
2 T. fresh chopped chives

In a large saucepan over medium heat, combine tomatoes, butter and crushed garlic. Simmer for about 30 minutes, until sauce has reduced. Stir in salt. Meanwhile, in a large pot of lightly salted boiling water, cook spaghetti until tender but firm. Drain well. In a large serving bowl, combine cooked spaghetti, sauce, grated Parmesan cheese and chopped chives.

Chicken Lasagna

Makes 12 servings

1 (1 lb.) pkg. fresh ground
   chicken
1 medium onion, chopped
1/2 C. chopped green bell
   peppers, optional
2 cloves garlic, minced
1 (30 oz.) jar spaghetti sauce
1 (15 oz.) container ricotta
   cheese

3/4 C. grated Parmesan
   cheese, divided
1 egg, beaten
1/4 tsp. pepper
9 lasagna noodles, cooked
3 1/2 C. shredded mozzarella
   cheese, divided

Preheat oven to 375°. In a large skillet over medium high heat, combine ground chicken, chopped onions, chopped green bell peppers and minced garlic. Heat until chicken is cooked throughout. Stir in sauce and cook until thoroughly heated and set aside. In a medium bowl, combine ricotta cheese, 1/2 cup grated Parmesan cheese, beaten egg and pepper. Mix well and set aside. Grease a 9x13" baking dish and spread 1/3 cup sauce mixture evenly across bottom of dish. Top with 3 cooked lasagna noodles. Spread 1/3 of the remaining sauce, 1/3 of the ricotta cheese mixture and 1 cup mozzarella cheese over noodles. Repeat layers with 3 noodles, 1/3 of the sauce mixture, 1/3 of the ricotta cheese mixture and 1 cup mozzarella cheese. Repeat layers again with remaining 3 noodles, remaining 1/3 sauce mixture and remaining 1/3 ricotta cheese mixture. Cover baking dish tightly with aluminum foil. Bake in oven for 40 minutes. Remove aluminum foil and top with remaining 1 1/2 cups mozzarella cheese and bake for an additional 15 minutes, until cheese is melted and bubbly.

Macaroni Pizza

Makes 5 servings

8 oz. elbow macaroni
1 egg, lightly beaten
1 1/2 C. shredded pizza-
    flavored cheese, divided
1/4 C. grated Parmesan cheese
1/2 tsp. salt
1/4 tsp. pepper

1/4 tsp. Italian seasoning
1/8 tsp. garlic powder
1 (14 oz.) jar pizza sauce
2 oz. pepperoni slices,
    optional
1 green pepper, diced

Preheat oven to 350°. In a large pot of lightly salted boiling water, cook elbow macaroni according to package directions. Drain pot. Grease a 12" round pizza pan and set aside. In a medium bowl, combine cooked macaroni, beaten egg, 1/2 cup shredded pizza-flavored cheese, grated Parmesan cheese, salt, pepper, Italian seasoning and garlic powder. Mix well. Carefully spoon the macaroni mixture onto the prepared pizza pan and spread evenly to make the crust. Spread pizza sauce evenly over macaroni mixture. Sprinkle remaining 1 cup pizza-flavored cheese, pepperoni slices and diced green peppers over sauce. Bake in oven for 20 minutes, until cheese is melted and crust is warmed.

Pasta Carbonara

Makes 8 servings

1/2 lb. bacon, cut into pieces
4 eggs, room temperature
1/4 C. heavy cream, room
    temperature
1 C. grated Parmesan cheese

16 oz. fettuccine
1/4 C. butter, softened
1/4 C. fresh chopped parsley
Pepper to taste

In a medium skillet over medium heat, cook bacon pieces until crisp. Drain bacon pieces on paper towels. In a medium bowl, beat together eggs and heavy cream just until blended. Stir in grated Parmesan cheese and set aside. In a large bowl of lightly salted boiling water, cook fettuccine according to package directions. Drain pot and return pasta to pan. Add butter and toss until butter is melted. Add cooked bacon and Parmesan cheese mixture. Toss until evenly coated. Season with pepper to taste.

Corn, Zucchini and Tomato Pie

Makes 6 to 8 servings

3 C. fresh or frozen corn
    kernels
5 small zucchini, cut into
    matchstick pieces
2 tsp. salt, divided
1 tsp. pepper, divided
1 T. dillweed

2 T. butter, melted
3 to 4 small tomatoes,
    cut into 1/2" slices
1/2 C. grated Parmesan
    cheese
1/4 C. dry bread crumbs
2 T. olive oil

Preheat oven to 375°. In a 9x13" glass baking dish, combine corn, zucchini pieces, 1 teaspoon salt, 1/2 teaspoon pepper, dillweed and melted butter. Toss until vegetables are thoroughly coated and spread evenly. Cover with tomato slices. Sprinkle tomato slices with remaining 1 teaspoon salt and remaining 1/2 teaspoon pepper. In a small bowl, combine grated Parmesan cheese and dry bread crumbs. Sprinkle bread crumbs mixture over tomatoes and drizzle casserole with olive oil. Bake in oven for 30 minutes, until cheese is bubbling. Remove from oven and let stand 5 minutes before serving.

Pork Dumplings

Makes 50 dumplings

1 lb. ground pork	1 1/2 T. sesame oil
1 1/2 tsp. fresh minced gingerroot	1 egg, beaten
2 cloves garlic, minced	5 C. finely shredded cabbage
1 T. thin sliced green onion	50 (3 1/2") square wonton wrappers
2 T. soy sauce	

In a large bowl, combine ground pork, minced gingerroot, minced garlic, sliced green onions, soy sauce, sesame oil, beaten egg and shredded cabbage. Mix well until evenly coated. Place 1 heaping teaspoon of pork filling onto each wonton wrapper. Moisten edges of wonton wrapper with water and fold edges up and over to form a triangle. Pinch edges slightly to seal the filling. To cook, steam dumplings over boiling water by placing in a vegetable steamer in a pot of boiling water or a bamboo steamer placed over a wok.

Grilled Barbecue Pizzas

Makes 4 individual pizzas

10 wooden skewers
1 yellow onion,
    cut into 1/2" slices
Olive oil
1/2 C. plus 2 T. barbecue
    sauce, divided

1 pkg. prepared pizza dough
6 oz. grilled pork or chicken,
    sliced thin
2 C. shredded Gouda or
    mozzarella cheese
1/4 C. fresh chopped cilantro

Preheat grill. Soak wooden skewers in hot water for 15 minutes. Insert wooden skewers into yellow onion slices from edges to prevent separating into rings. Brush onions lightly with olive oil. Grill onions for 20 to 30 minutes, until tender. Brush 2 tablespoons barbecue sauce over onions for last 5 minutes of grilling time. Remove onions from grill. Remove wooden skewers from onions, separate into rings and set aside. Separate prepared pizza dough into 4 round balls. Roll or gently stretch each ball into a 7" round. Brush rounds lightly on both sides with olive oil. Place dough rounds on grill for about 1 to 3 minutes, until lightly browned. Turn crusts and grill other side for 3 to 5 minutes. Remove crusts from grill and brush one side of each pizza with remaining 1/2 cup barbecue sauce. Top each pizza with grilled pork slices, onion rings, shredded cheese and chopped cilantro. Return pizzas to grill for about 5 minutes, until bottom of crusts are crisp and cheese is melted.

Chicken & Pasta Toss

Makes 3 to 4 servings

**2 cooked chicken breast
    halves**
**1 (9 oz.) pkg. plain or
    lemon-pepper flavored
    linguine**
1/4 C. olive oil
**1/2 medium yellow onion,
    sliced**

3 cloves garlic, minced
**1 C. sautéed red or yellow
    bell pepper slices**
**1/4 C. fresh chopped basil
    or parsley**
1 C. grated Parmesan cheese
Salt and pepper to taste

Cut cooked chicken breast halves into thin slices. In a large pot of lightly salted boiling water, cook linguine according to package directions until al dente. Drain pot and place linguine in a large serving bowl. Set aside and keep warm. In a large skillet over medium heat, heat olive oil. Add sliced onions and minced garlic to skillet and cook until tender but crisp. Add sliced cooked chicken, onion and garlic mixture, sautéed bell pepper slices, chopped basil and grated Parmesan cheese to linguine. Season with salt and pepper to taste. Toss until well mixed.

Perfectly Grilled
Steak & Potatoes

Makes 4 servings

Olive oil
1 1/2 tsp. cracked black
   pepper
2 cloves garlic, pressed
Salt
1/2 tsp. dried thyme

4 beef tenderloin steaks or
   boneless top loin steaks,
   cut 1 1/2" thick
4 medium potatoes,
   cut into 1/2" slices
Pepper to taste
Lime wedges, optional

   Preheat grill and lightly oil the grate. Cover half of the grate with aluminum foil. Drizzle olive oil over the aluminum foil. In a small bowl, combine 2 tablespoons olive oil, cracked black pepper, pressed garlic, 1/2 teaspoon salt and dried thyme. Mix well and brush over steaks to coat both sides. Brush potato slices with additional olive oil and season to taste with salt and pepper. Grill steaks on oiled grate for 10 to 12 minutes for medium-rare or to desired doneness, turning once. Place sliced potatoes on aluminum foil and grill for 10 to 12 minutes or until potatoes are golden brown and tender, turning once. To serve, place 1 steak and 1/4 of the potatoes on each of the 4 serving plates. If desired, garnish with lime wedges.

Polish Cabbage Noodles

Makes 5 to 6 servings

1 (16 oz.) pkg. wide egg noodles
1/2 C. butter

1 medium heat cabbage, shredded
2 red onions, cut into strips
Salt and pepper to taste

In a large pot of lightly salted water, cook egg noodles according to package directions. In a large skillet over medium heat, melt butter. Add shredded cabbage and onion strips and sauté until tender. Drain pasta and return to pot. Add sautéed cabbage and onions to noodles and toss until evenly coated. Season with salt and pepper to taste.

Pasta 'All Amatriciana' with Artichokes & Olives

Makes 6 servings

4 oz. pancetta or lightly
   smoked bacon, diced
3 large cloves garlic, minced
2 (14 1/2 oz.) cans diced
   tomatoes with oil,
   garlic and onions
1 (14 oz.) can artichoke
   hearts, drained and
   quartered

1/2 C. dry white wine
1 (2 oz.) can sliced olives,
   drained
2 T. fresh chopped rosemary
1/4 tsp. crushed red pepper
1/4 C. fresh chopped parsley
1 lb. fettuccine or linguine
Salt and pepper to taste

In a large skillet over medium high heat, cook pancetta
for about 6 minutes, until browned. Add minced garlic
and continue cooking for 30 seconds, stirring frequently.
Add tomatoes with oil, garlic and onions, quartered
artichoke hearts, white wine, sliced olives, chopped
rosemary and crushed red pepper. Reduce heat to medium
low and let simmer for 10 minutes, stirring occasionally.
Stir in chopped parsley. Meanwhile, in a large pot of
lightly salted boiling water, cook pasta about 10 minutes,
until tender but firm. Drain pot and return pasta to pot.
Add sauce mixture and toss until pasta is evenly coated.
Season with salt and pepper to taste. If desired, garnish
with additional rosemary.

Creamy Pasta Bake

Makes 10 servings

1 (30 oz.) jar spaghetti sauce
1 (16 oz.) pkg. rotini pasta,
   cooked and drained
1 1/2 C. sour cream

1 (10 oz.) pkg. frozen
   chopped spinach,
   thawed and drained
1/2 C. grated Parmesan
   cheese

Preheat oven to 375°. In a large bowl, combine spaghetti sauce, cooked rotini pasta, sour cream, drained chopped spinach and grated Parmesan cheese. Mix well and transfer mixture to a greased 9x13" baking dish. Bake in oven for 25 minutes.

Cheeseburger Macaroni

1/2 lb. ground beef
2 1/4 C. water
1/2 C. ketchup
1 tsp. prepared mustard,
    optional

2 C. elbow macaroni
3/4 lb. Velveeta cheese,
    cubed

In a large skillet over medium high heat, brown ground beef. Drain skillet of fat and add water, ketchup and mustard. Bring to a boil and stir in macaroni. Reduce heat to medium low, cover and let simmer for 8 to 10 minutes until macaroni is tender. Add cubed Velveeta cheese and stir until melted.

Seasoned Pork Chops

Makes 6 servings

2 (1 oz.) pkgs. dry onion soup mix	1 (4 1/2 oz.) can mushrooms, drained
3 C. water	Salt and pepper to taste
2 C. instant rice	6 pork chops, cut 3/4" thick

Preheat oven to 350°. In a medium bowl, combine dry onion soup mix and water, mixing until soup mix is dissolved. Pour mixture into a 10x15" baking dish. Add instant rice and drained mushrooms and mix well. Add salt and pepper to taste. Lay pork chops over mixture in baking dish. Push pork chops into mixture and spoon mixture over pork chops. Cover baking dish tightly with aluminum foil and bake in oven for 1 hour.

Pasta Lasagna

Makes 5 servings

1/2 lb. penne pasta	2 C. shredded mozzarella
1/2 lb. lean ground beef	cheese, divided
1 (26 oz.) jar pasta sauce	1/4 C. grated Parmesan
1 (15 oz.) container ricotta	cheese
cheese	1 egg, beaten

Preheat oven to 350°. Grease a 2 1/2 quart baking dish and set aside. In a large pot of lightly salted boiling water, cook pasta for 8 to 10 minutes, until tender but firm. Drain pot and set pasta aside. In a large skillet over medium heat, cook ground beef until browned. Drain skillet of fat and add pasta sauce. Remove from heat and mix well. In a medium bowl, combine ricotta cheese, 1 cup shredded mozzarella cheese, grated Parmesan cheese and beaten egg. Mix until well combined. Spread half of the cooked pasta evenly across bottom of prepared dish. Top with half of the sauce mixture and half of the cheese mixture. Repeat layers with remaining half of the noodles, remaining half of the sauce mixture and remaining half of the cheese mixture. Top with remaining 1 cup mozzarella cheese. Bake in oven for 35 to 40 minutes, until lasagna is hot and bubbly.

Chicken & Dumplings

Makes 6 to 8 servings

4 lbs. whole chicken,
   cut apart
1 dried red chili pepper,
   seeded and diced
2 carrots, chopped
2 stalks celery, chopped
2 onions, chopped
1 bay leaf

3 cloves garlic, minced
4 (14 1/2 oz.) cans chicken
   broth
2 C. heavy cream, divided
1/4 C. cornstarch
1/2 C. water
2 C. flour

In a large pot over high heat, combine chicken parts, diced chili peppers, chopped carrots, chopped celery, chopped onions, bay leaf, minced garlic and chicken broth. Mix well and bring to a boil. Reduce heat to low, cover and let simmer for 1 to 2 hours, until chicken comes off bones easily. Cover and refrigerate overnight. Skim fat from top of soup and remove chicken parts. Remove chicken from bones and chop remaining meat into small pieces and set aside. Using a slotted spoon, remove vegetables from soup and discard. Return pot to stove and cook over high heat. Bring to a boil, reduce heat and let simmer for 10 to 15 minutes. Add 1 cup heavy cream and mix well. In a small bowl, combine cornstarch and water. Add cornstarch mixture to pot. Stir until thickened. In a large bowl, combine flour and remaining 1 cup heavy cream. Mix well and roll dough into 1 1/2" balls. Drop balls carefully into the simmering soup and cook for about 7 minutes. Cover soup and continue cooking for 7 minutes. Add chicken pieces and mix well. Cook until chicken is heated throughout.

Chicken Marsala

Makes 4 servings

1 lb. boneless, skinless chicken breast halves	2/3 C. dry Marsala wine
1 1/4 tsp. olive oil	1/2 C. chicken broth
3/4 medium onion, chopped	2 tsp. cornstarch
	Salt and pepper to taste

Pound chicken breast halves to 1/4" thickness. In a large skillet over medium high heat, heat olive oil. Add chopped onions and sauté for 5 minutes. Add chicken breast halves and cook on each side for 5 minutes. Add Marsala wine and cook for 4 minutes or until wine is the consistency of syrup. In a small bowl, combine chicken broth and cornstarch. Add cornstarch mixture to skillet and cook for 2 minutes, until the sauce is thickened. Add salt and pepper to taste.

Vegetable Spaghetti

Makes 4 servings

1/2 lb. spaghetti
4 medium yellow squash,
    cut into small slices
4 medium zucchini,
    cut into small slices

1/4 C. grated Parmesan
    cheese
2 C. tomato pasta sauce

In a large pot of lightly salted boiling water, cook spaghetti for 7 to 10 minutes until tender. Drain well and return spaghetti to pot. Add sliced squash, sliced zucchini, grated Parmesan cheese and tomato pasta sauce. Mix until evenly coated.

Sweet & Sour Chicken

Makes 4 servings

2 tsp. olive oil	1 tomato, cut into 1" cubes
1 onion, cut into slivers	1 C. Chinese duck sauce or
1 sweet green pepper, cored,	apricot basting sauce
seeded and cut into	1 T. ketchup
1/2" squares	1 T. cider vinegar
3/4 lb. boneless, skinless	2 tsp. soy sauce
chicken breasts, cut into	2 tsp. cornstarch
3/4" wide strips	1 T. water

In a large nonstick skillet over medium heat, heat olive oil. Add onion pieces and sauté for 2 minutes. Add green pepper pieces and sauté for an additional 3 minutes. Increase heat to medium high. Stir in chicken pieces and sauté for 5 minutes, until cooked throughout. Stir in tomatoes, duck sauce, ketchup, cider vinegar and soy sauce. In a small bowl, dissolve cornstarch in 1 tablespoon water. Add cornstarch mixture to skillet. Bring to a boil. Cook, stirring often, until thickened, about 1 minute.

Scalloped Potato & Roasted Red Pepper Bake

Makes 6 to 8 servings

3 T. butter or margarine	2 T. fresh chopped parsley
1 large onion, chopped	6 medium potatoes, peeled
3 T. flour	1 (7 oz.) jar roasted red sweet
1/4 tsp. salt	peppers, drained and
1/4 tsp. pepper	chopped
2 C. milk	Fresh rosemary or parsley
1 C. shredded Swiss or	sprigs, optional
Gruyere cheese	

Preheat oven to 350°. In a large saucepan over medium heat, melt butter and sauté onions until tender, being careful not to brown. Stir in flour, salt and pepper. Add milk and cook over medium heat, stirring frequently, until thickened and bubbly. Remove from heat and stir in shredded cheese and chopped parsley, until cheese is melted. Slice potatoes very thin. Grease a 2 quart baking dish and cover the bottom evenly with half of the potatoes. Cover with half of the onions mixture. Layer chopped roasted red peppers over onions mixture. Cover with remaining half of the potatoes and remaining half of the onions mixture. Bake in oven for 1 hour and 15 minutes. Uncover and bake an additional 15 minutes, until potatoes are tender. If desired, garnish with fresh rosemary or parsley sprigs.

Chicken Enchiladas

Makes 5 servings

1 T. vegetable oil
1 medium onion, chopped
1 clove garlic, minced
1 (4 oz.) can chopped green
    chilies, drained
3 C. shredded cooked
    chicken

1 (10 oz.) can mild enchilada
    sauce
2 C. shredded Pepper-Jack
    cheese, divided
10 (6") corn tortillas
1 C. half n' half

Preheat oven to 375°. In a large nonstick skillet over medium heat, heat vegetable oil. Add chopped onions and minced garlic and sauté for about 5 minutes. Add chopped green chilies, shredded cooked chicken and enchilada sauce, cooking for 2 minutes. Stir in 1/2 cup shredded Pepper-Jack cheese and remove from heat. Grease a 9x13" baking dish and set aside. Wrap tortillas in damp paper towels and heat in microwave for 1 minute. Dip each tortilla in warm water, shaking off excess. Fill each tortilla with 1/3 cup chicken mixture. Roll up tortillas and place, seam side down, in prepared pan. Cover enchiladas with half n' half and sprinkle with remaining 1 1/2 cups shredded cheese. Bake in oven for 10 minutes. Adjust oven temperature to broil. Broil enchiladas for 5 minutes, until golden brown.

Baked Macaroni

Makes 6 to 8 servings

1 lb. ground beef
1 (1 lb.) pkg. elbow
   macaroni, cooked
1 medium onion, chopped

1 can tomato soup
1 can vegetable soup
Salt and pepper to taste

Preheat oven to 350°. In a deep 9x13" baking dish, spread ground beef evenly across bottom. Add cooked macaroni and chopped onions and mix well. Add tomato soup and mix well. Add vegetable soup and mix well. Season with salt and pepper to taste. Bake in oven for 45 to 60 minutes, until ground beef is cooked and top of casserole is crispy.

Gulasch (German Stew)

Makes 4 servings

1 C. butter, divided
1 tsp. minced garlic
1 medium onion, sliced
1 green bell pepper,
    sliced lengthwise
1 red bell pepper,
    sliced lengthwise
1 1/2 lbs. stew meat,
    cut into 1" cubes

4 T. flour
4 C. beef broth
4 oz. sour cream
1 tsp. salt
1/2 tsp. pepper
1 tsp. paprika
1 tsp. dried oregano
1 C. fresh mushrooms,
    chopped
1 C. medium egg noodles

In a large soup pot over medium heat, melt 1/2 cup butter and sauté minced garlic and sliced onions for about 5 minutes, stirring occasionally. Add sliced green and red bell peppers and sauté for an additional 5 minutes. Using a slotted spoon, remove sautéed vegetables from pot and set aside. Add cubed stew meat to soup pot and brown on all sides. Sprinkle flour over stew meat and stir until coated. Quickly add beef broth and mix well. Add sour cream, salt, pepper, paprika and dried oregano. Return sautéed vegetables to pot, cover and bring to a boil. Reduce heat and simmer for 30 minutes, stirring occasionally. In a separate pot of lightly salted boiling water, cook egg noodles according to package directions. Drain pot and set egg noodles aside. In a medium saucepan, melt remaining 1/2 cup butter and sauté mushrooms for 5 to 10 minutes. When stew is fully cooked, add mushrooms and return to a boil. Simmer for an additional 3 to 5 minutes, stirring occasionally. Serve stew over cooked egg noodles.

Vegetable Turkey Noodle Soup

2 lbs. ground turkey
3 large onions, chopped
2 T. minced garlic
1 (1/3 lb.) box pasta shells
4 T. curry powder
2 qts. tomato pasta sauce

4 C. chopped carrots
4 C. chopped broccoli
4 C. sliced celery
4 C. chopped cauliflower
2 cans green beans

In a large saucepan over medium high heat, brown ground turkey. Add chopped onions and minced garlic and sauté until onions are tender. In a large pot of lightly salted boiling water, cook pasta shells according to package directions. Drain pot and return pasta to pot. Add ground turkey and sautéed onions and garlic. Add curry powder, pasta sauce, chopped carrots, chopped broccoli, sliced celery, chopped cauliflower and green beans. Mix well and simmer for 15 minutes, until heated throughout. Remove from heat and let stand 15 minutes before serving.

Veggie Soup with Pasta

Makes 6 servings

2 (14 oz.) can beef broth
1 (16 oz.) pkg. frozen mixed
    vegetables
1 C. frozen French-cut
    green beans
1 C. chopped summer squash
2 tsp. dried basil
1/4 tsp. crushed red pepper
    flakes

1/4 tsp. garlic salt
1 (14 1/2 oz.) can whole
    tomatoes in juice
10 oz. angel hair pasta,
    broken
2 T. grated Parmesan cheese
1 T. fresh chopped parsley,
    optional

In a large saucepan over medium heat, combine beef broth, frozen mixed vegetables, French-cut green beans, summer squash, dried basil, crushed red pepper flakes and garlic salt. Bring mixture to a boil, reduce heat, cover and let simmer for about 7 to 8 minutes. In a blender, puree whole tomatoes in juice. Add pureed tomatoes to mixture and cook until heated throughout. Meanwhile, in a large pot of lightly salted boiling water, cook angel hair pasta according to package directions. Drain pot and divide pasta evenly into 6 serving bowls. Spoon vegetable mixture over the pasta in each bowl. Sprinkle grated Parmesan cheese over vegetable mixture. If desired, garnish with chopped parsley.

Creamy Wild Rice Soup

Makes 4 servings

1 (10 1/2 oz.) can cream of
   celery soup
10 1/2 oz. skim milk
10 1/2 oz. Velveeta cheese,
   cubed

1 1/2 C. cooked wild rice
1 (6 1/2 oz.) can mushrooms,
   drained
1/2 to 1 C. chopped carrots
1/2 C. sliced almonds

In a slow cooker on high, place cream of celery soup.
Add skim milk and heat, stirring frequently. Add cubed
Velveeta cheese and continue to stir. When Velveeta is
almost melted, add cooked wild rice, drained mushrooms,
chopped carrots and sliced almonds. Continue to cook
until soup is heated throughout.

Mexi-Chicken Soup

Makes 8 servings

3 (13 3/4 oz.) cans chicken
   broth
1 (15 1/4 oz.) can whole corn
   kernels, drained
1 (14 1/2 oz.) can diced
   tomatoes, drained

1 (15 oz.) can red kidney
   beans, drained
1 lb. boneless, skinless
   chicken breasts,
   cut into small pieces

In a large saucepan over medium heat, combine
chicken broth, corn, diced tomatoes, kidney beans and
chicken pieces. Bring to a boil, stirring
occasionally. Cook soup for 5
minutes and remove from heat.
Cover saucepan and let stand for
15 minutes.

Beef & Barley Soup

Makes 4 servings

1 T. vegetable oil
1 1/4 lbs. boneless sirloin
    steak, cut into 3/4" cubes
1 (13 3/4 oz.) can beef broth

3/4 C. quick-cooking barley
5 C. water
1 (10 oz.) pkg. frozen mixed
    vegetables

In a large saucepan over medium high heat, heat vegetable oil. Add beef cubes in batches, sautéing until browned, about 4 minutes per batch. As batches are browned, transfer to a pie plate or bowl. Return all browned beef to saucepan and add beef broth, barley and water. Bring to a boil. Reduce heat, cover and let simmer for 10 minutes, until barley is tender. Stir in frozen mixed vegetables and cook for 5 minutes, until heated throughout.

Italian Vegetable Rice Soup

Makes 4 servings

1 qt. plus 2 C. vegetable or
    chicken
2 carrots, peeled and diced
1 zucchini, diced
1 lb. canned Great Northern
    beans in juice

1 1/2 C. instant rice
1 tsp. Italian seasoning
1/4 C. grated Parmesan
    cheese

In a large saucepan over high heat, bring broth and diced carrots to a boil. Add diced zucchini, Great Northern beans in juice, instant rice and Italian seasoning. Cook about 5 minutes, until vegetables are tender. Before serving, sprinkle with grated Parmesan cheese.

Southwestern Corn Chowder

Makes 8 servings

3 slices bacon, diced
1/2 C. chopped onions
1 C. finely chopped sweet
    red pepper
2 large potatoes, peeled
    and cubed
1 (4 1/2 oz.) can chopped
    green chilies, drained

6 C. chicken broth
2 (10 oz.) pkgs. frozen corn
    kernels
1/2 tsp. salt
1/4 tsp. cayenne pepper
1/4 C. half n' half
2 T. fresh chopped cilantro,
    optional

In a large saucepan over medium high heat, sauté diced bacon and chopped onions, about 5 minutes, until onion is softened and lightly browned. Add chopped sweet red pepper and sauté for an additional minute. Add cubed potatoes and drained chilies and cook for 5 minutes, stirring frequently. Add chicken broth, corn, salt and cayenne pepper. Reduce heat to medium, cover and let simmer for 15 minutes, until potatoes are fork tender. Transfer half of the soup to a food processor or blender. Puree and return to saucepan. Stir in half n' half and remove from heat. If desired, add chopped cilantro.

Delicious Ham & Potato Soup

Makes 8 servings

3 1/2 C. peeled, diced potatoes
1/3 C. diced celery
1/3 C. finely chopped onions
3/4 C. cooked, diced ham
3 1/4 C. water
2 T. chicken bouillon
    granules

1/2 tsp. salt
1 tsp. white or black pepper
5 T. butter
5 T. flour
2 C. milk

In a large stock pot over medium heat, combine diced potatoes, diced celery, chopped onions, diced ham and water. Bring to a boil, reduce heat and simmer for about 10 to 15 minutes or until potatoes are tender. Add chicken bouillon, salt and pepper and mix well. In a separate saucepan over medium low heat, melt butter. Whisk in flour and cook for about 1 minute, stirring constantly, until thickened. Slowly stir in milk, making sure no lumps are formed. Continue cooking for 4 to 5 minutes, until thickened. Add milk mixture to stock pot and cook until soup is heated throughout. Serve immediately.

Index

Desserts

Main Dish & Soups